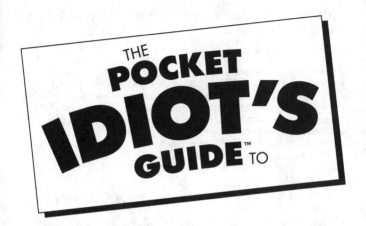

THE
POCKET
IDIOT'S
GUIDE™ TO

Freshwater Aquariums

by Mike Wickham

alpha
books

A Division of Macmillan General Reference
A Pearson Education Macmillan Company
1633 Broadway, New York, NY 10019-6785

To my parents, who have always been my biggest fans, and to Mother Nature.

©1999 Mike Wickham

THE POCKET IDIOT'S GUIDE TO & Design are registered trademarks of Macmillan, Inc.

Macmillan General Reference books may be purchased for business or sales promotional use. For information please write: Special Markets Department, Macmillan Publishing USA, 1633 Broadway, New York, NY 10019-6785.

International Standard Book Number: ISBN 1-58245-110-9
Library of Congress Catalog Card Number: 99-61201

01   00   99   8   7   6   5   4   3   2   1

Interpretation of the printing code: the rightmost number of the first series of numbers is the year of the book's printing; the rightmost number of the second series of numbers is the number of the book's printing. For example, a printing code of 99-1 shows that the first printing occurred in 1999.

Printed in the United States of America

Note: This publication contains the opinions and ideas of its author. It is intended to provide helpful and informative material on the subject matter covered. It is sold with the understanding that the author and publisher are not engaged in rendering professional services in the book. If the reader requires personal assistance or advice, a competent professional should be consulted.

The author and publisher specifically disclaim any responsibility for any liability, loss or risk, personal or otherwise, which is incurred as a consequence, directly or indirectly, of the use and application of any of the contents of this book.

Alpha Development Team

Publisher
Kathy Nebenhaus

Editorial Director
Gary M. Krebs

Managing Editor
Bob Shuman

Marketing Brand Manager
Felice Primeau

Acquisitions Editor
Jessica Faust

Development Editors
Phil Kitchel
Amy Zavatto

Assistant Editor
Georgette Blau

Production Team

Editors
Beth Adelman
Don Stevens

Production Editor
Kristi Hart

Cover Designer
Mike Freeland

Cartoonist
Kevin Spear

Photos and Illustrations
Mike Wickham

Book Designers
Scott Cook and Amy Adams of DesignLab

Indexer
Johnna Van Hoose

Production Team
Ellen Considine
Marie Kristine Parial-Leonardo

Contents at a Glance

Introduction

How to Use This Book

As you read *The Pocket Idiot's Guide to Freshwater Aquariums,* you will soon recognize that it is very much like your aquarium—it is structured like an ecosystem. In an ecosystem, if you change a parameter (by adding or removing a species, for example), it will affect something else. Everything is interconnected.

The information in this book is very similar. Just about every fact in every chapter relates in some way to the information in other chapters. Skip something and you may change the complete picture in your tank. Change something and you may find unexpected consequences. It's a ripple effect.

How much would you pay for a book like this? You might expect to pay a jillion dollars, but not with this special offer! But, wait . . . don't get out your checkbook yet, because there's more! That's right! If you act today, I'll also throw in a table of contents, an index, and several informative . . .

Boxes! They give you extra pointers by highlighting various important and interesting tidbits of information. Watch for these boxes:

Fish and Tips

Check here for helpful hints that save you time and money, and make fishkeeping easier.

Fish School

Look here for definitions of unfamiliar words.

Something's Fishy

When something is not quite right, we say that something's fishy. These boxes contain warnings and safety tips.

Trademarks

All terms mentioned in this book that are known to be or are suspected of being trademarks or service marks have been appropriately capitalized. Alpha books and Macmillan General Reference cannot attest to the accuracy of this information. Use of a term in this book should not be regarded as affecting the validity of any trademark or service mark.

Chapter 1

What Kind of Tank Do You Want?

In This Chapter

➤ Why bigger is better

➤ Big fish, little fish

➤ Mother Nature vs. polypropylene

The first step in planning your tank is deciding what size fish you plan to keep. Big fish eat little fish. With rare exceptions, you cannot mix large fish with small ones. That is, not unless you want the small fish to be bait for the lunkers—the big fish in your small pond.

Fishy snacks aside, the size of fish you keep will determine what size aquarium you need to buy. Do you want to keep small fish? If so, you can keep a few in a small aquarium, or many in a large tank. However, if you want to keep jumbo fish, you will need to buy a large tank right off the bat.

Something's Fishy

Big fish eat little fish. Even big *peaceful* fish eat little fish.

You cannot crowd your fish, or they will die. Big fish require more gallons of water per inch of fish. In Chapter 7 on picking your first fish, I will give you some detailed guidelines on how to determine how many fish will fit in your tank. Those guidelines can also help you determine what size tank to buy.

Peaceful Community or Wrestling Ring

Some people like to watch fish to relax. They like to view the graceful movements and enjoy the ebb and flow of motion. The serenity attracts them.

I fall into that category. I prefer to see the plants swaying in the current, schools of fish flitting by like a flock of birds, and catfish grazing along the bottom like contented cows. I like my aquariums to be pastoral, even when I plant them like a jungle. Yes, the community tank is for me. It also happens that the community tank is what most people keep.

Fish School

An aquarium containing a mixture of small peaceful fish is called a *community tank*.

Other people prefer action and drama. They want to see an assault here and there, and maybe even some serious bloodshed. Aggressive fish have evolved to behave that way, so there is nothing wrong with keeping them and enjoying them for doing what they do naturally. One thing about Mother Nature is that she offers it all, and it is no different in the aquarium. A tank can be set up to provide this kind of setting, too.

Do You Want to Fool Mother Nature?

How do you visualize your aquarium? Is it filled with driftwood, natural rocks and gravel, and live plants swaying in the current? Or do you prefer having a six-inch plastic diver bubbling next to a four-inch plastic shipwreck, with plastic palm trees sprouting stiffly from fluorescent pink gravel?

Seriously, everyone has their own preferences. It is your tank, so you get to decide how it will be decorated. Don't let anyone berate your choice of decorations, no matter how strange or silly they are. But choosing between natural decorations and artificial ones is a choice you must make.

Obviously, my preference is for the natural aquarium. I am a bit of a purist; I like my aquariums to look like something you might find in nature. To my knowledge, fish have not evolved to enjoy living around fluorescent pink gravel and plants they can't eat. I prefer to set up my aquariums in a way that is most likely to make the fish feel at home. An advantage of this is that the fish feel more secure and show their coloration to the fullest.

But this is America, and when that guy in *The Graduate* said he could sum up the future in one word—plastics—he wasn't far off the mark. In fact, if you want, you can buy every kind of decoration in plastic. There are plastic plants, plastic rocks, pieces of plastic driftwood, and of course, plastic castles and treasure chests. You can even buy plastic fish. Heck, even Goofy and Mickey Mouse are available in diving gear to decorate and aerate your tank.

Plastic Pluses and Minuses

The heavily planted style aquarium and the one that relies on plastic each have their advantages and disadvantages.

Plastic rocks and driftwood won't leach any substances into the water, so you don't have to worry about them changing the pH or hardness of your water, and some plastic rocks even lock together so that you don't have to worry about them caving in on your fish.

Plastic plants don't die and they don't need to be trimmed. There is no need to worry about how much light they get, or to bother offering fertilizer to them. All in all, they are fairly maintenance free. But the downside is that they don't compete with algae for nutrients, so you are more likely to have algae to scrub in a tank that has plastic plants instead of live ones.

Fish and Tips

The kind of fish you keep may influence your decor choices. If you keep large fish that like to dig, you will have a hard time keeping live plants with them. Plastic plants may work better, because they can stand continual abuse and uprooting.

While plastic plants may not die, they also do not grow. Once you set up a scene, there is nothing dynamic about it. Unless you physically move the plants around, you will have a static display. Every leaf will be in the same place tomorrow as it is today.

Of course, live plants do have some disadvantages. They may shed some leaves, giving you a bit more debris to clear away. Also, they may grow to the point where you need to spend time pruning and replanting. (However, if you give your plants proper care, you may be able to sell extras back to your dealer for credit on supplies.) And, of course, if you do things wrong, live plants may rot and die. Some fish love to eat plants, too. If you plan to keep a tank full of silver dollars, for example, you may find that plastic plants serve you better.

Mix It Up

Another option is to mix. Often, aquarists will have both live and plastic plants in their tanks. Plastic plants are used in place of delicate species, or instead of species that are easily munched. It is a useful compromise that lets the live-plant-loving aquarist enjoy species he or she might otherwise be unable to keep.

By the way, most of the plastic plants sold in aquarium stores are fashioned after actual species of aquatic plants. You also will probably find nonaquatic species such as plastic marijuana plants, and stuff like that. Hey, they may not be aquarium plants, but if customers buy them, dealers happily line up to sell them. You can't blame a dealer for finding a way to take your money.

Whether you go plastic or *au naturel*, you will create a habitat for your fish. So let's talk about some of the various habitats you can establish in your tank.

Aquariums with Style

Obviously, there are many ways to set up an aquarium, and you need to pick what suits you best. Here are some typical styles of freshwater aquaria that might fit your needs.

Heavily Planted

This is my favorite style. I like to make my tank look like a jungle, with some room left over for the fish to swim. Mixing in a few rocks and pieces of driftwood makes an even more natural appearance. Admittedly, a similar decor can be set up using plastic plants, and some look quite nice, but that isn't for me.

Rock Pile

This style is especially popular with African cichlid fans. Few, if any, plants are put in the aquarium. These fish tend to eat most plants, anyway. Instead, a large thick, wall of rocks is built, with plenty of shelves, ledges, caves, and holes. The fish chase each other in and out all day, and the tank is always full of action.

Wide Open Spaces

Some hobbyists go very light on the decorations and leave lots of swimming space. Usually, this style of tank looks naked to me, but there are times when it has its uses. Large fish may constantly knock over and move decorations around the tank, especially species that dig a lot. In that situation, the plants would all end up floating and the rocks would all end up buried by gravel, anyway.

When it comes right down to it, though, all tanks should have some wide open space. If you put plants and rocks right up to the glass, you may not get to see the fish much. And if you keep schooling fish, they like to have some space to chase each other around.

Theme Tanks

This often grotesque category can contain a real hodge-podge of styles. A popular version would have several aerating ornaments with a common theme bubbling away. Or, it may be something as simple as setting up a tank that only contains species of rainbows or barbs. I've seen theme tanks set up with assorted plastic divers doing various treasure-hunting chores. Piranha tanks with piles of ceramic skulls in them are a popular choice. I even have seen patriotic theme tanks that had red, white, and blue plastic plants as the only decor.

Chapter 2

Finding a Qualified Dealer

In This Chapter

➤ How to determine if your dealer is a doofus

➤ Learn which is more important: quality, selection, or price

➤ I tell you where to go . . . shopping

➤ Understanding guarantees

You can make it easier on yourself if you find a good place to shop—a place with helpful, knowledgeable staff. Your dealer can play a big part in your success. It is important to find a dealer who can serve your needs, and is willing to do so.

Now, some of you won't be lucky. You will find yourselves living in towns that are too small to support more than one pet store or aquarium shop. You may have to travel some distance to find just one store to serve your needs, and even then, the selection might be quite limited.

Many of you will be much luckier. If you live in a major metropolitan area, you are likely to find many stores where you can buy fish, aquariums, and supplies. You will find a better selection, and more competitive prices. Lucky you.

But whether you live in the city or a rural area, you need to find a good dealer. You need to find someone who sells the equipment you need, who stocks the fish you covet, and who can offer advice when you need it. You need to find a dealer who you can think of as a friend in the business.

How do you find such a person? I'm glad you asked.

Dead Fish Stink

I put this at the top of my list, and for a very good reason. A dealer whose tanks have many dead fish is a dealer who probably doesn't know how to properly care for them. If he can't keep his own fish alive, how is he going to be able to offer advice that you can trust to keep your fish alive? Further, do you want to risk buying from tanks that are full of dead and diseased fish?

Avoid stores where there are lots of dead fish. They are bad news, pure and simple. Now, having said that, let me qualify this a little. Fish are livestock. Livestock is perishable. That means fish can die. Eventually, even healthy fish will die—of old age or accident, or maybe some other healthy fish will decide to have them for lunch or beat them to death. So it is unreasonable to expect that you will never see a dead fish in your dealer's tanks, even if he is the best dealer in the whole wide fishy world.

Fresh Fish

Avoid buying new arrivals. Your dealer has new shipments of fish coming in all the time, and that means he has new shipments of stressed-out fish arriving constantly. Stressed fish are fish that tend to get sick.

Imagine being crammed into a plastic bag with up to a thousand other fish, and then put into a dark box that gets tossed around, roasted, and chilled in transit. Imagine being locked up that way, without food, for up to 48 hours. That is what many fish go through to get from fish farms in Asia to the tank in your home. Worse, they may have stressful stops on the way as they pass through the hands of transshippers and wholesalers. The result is that some fish will get sick, especially if they are new arrivals.

Now, you are not going to be able to tell if a fish is a new arrival by looking at it—at least, not unless you are in the store so often that you can recognize a tank of fish that wasn't there previously. So the only way to know how long a fish has been in your dealer's stock is to ask. The longer your dealer has had a fish in stock, the safer it will be to buy it.

Do not buy from medicated tanks. Your dealer may treat tanks because the fish in them are obviously sick, or he may medicate new arrivals solely as a preventive. While it is true that fish receiving preventive medication are probably completely fine, you still should not buy from those tanks.

Look for the Good Stuff, Too

Don't just look for dead fish. Your dealer may be lousy at keeping fish alive but very good at regularly searching out and discarding dead bodies. So it is also important to look for healthy stock. Look for fish with bright eyes and erect fins. Look for fish with energy.

Look for fish with an interest in life. When you approach the tank, do they come running for food? Now, you may think this is a bad sign, because they act like they are starving. But the fact that they swim toward you, hoping for food, is a good sign they are well fed—that they get fed often enough to have learned that when people approach, munchies may be approaching, too.

Fish and Tips

Dedicated pet and aquarium stores are usually much better sources for quality stock and supplies than are stores that simply wedge a pet department in between the shoes and the sporting goods.

Feel free to stick your hand near the front glass to see if the fish come running. However, please do not touch the glass or tap on it. Sound travels through water much easier than it travels through air. So tapping on the glass is like unexpectedly crashing cymbals in a fish's ears. It can frighten a fish very badly, and can cause injury. Besides, touching the glass leaves finger marks that make it harder to see the fish.

A Predilection for Large Selection

There are thousands of species of fish available in the hobby. Your dealer won't be able to carry them all, but the more tanks he has, the better his selection will be.

A large aquarium store is likely to have a large selection, making shopping more fun, but don't overlook the small stores. The most important consideration is the health of the livestock. Sometimes the largest store around has the most disease-ridden fish, because they are just too busy or lacking in expertise to give the fish the proper care.

Look for a large selection of dry goods, too. Does the dealer carry more than one brand of various items? It is good to see some choices. A dealer who carries only one brand for most items is a dealer who doesn't understand that everyone's needs are not the same. Your dealer's recommendations are going to be very valuable, but there still should be some flexibility.

Ask the Experts

Your dealer can't help you if he doesn't know what he is doing. As a novice to the hobby, you are at a disadvantage because you don't know what you are doing, either.

How can you tell if your particular salesperson knows his stuff? Arm yourself with a little knowledge beforehand. The more you know before you walk into a store, the better you will be able to judge what kind of advice you are getting. Since you are reading this book, I would say it's safe to assume you are already arming yourself with knowledge. If you at least know the basics, you will be able to tell if the information given to you by a salesperson agrees with what you already know.

Fortunately, the odds are good that the employees will at least know the basics. So even if you get a rookie to wait on you, you probably will be okay. However, if you feel a salesperson is not yet ready to answer your questions, don't be afraid to ask if there is someone with more experience available to help you—even if you have to come back later.

As you get answers to your questions, listen to how they are delivered. Does the person have an answer for everything? This may indicate a salesperson who likes to bluff his way through a conversation. You need someone who is willing to admit when he doesn't know something. Does the salesperson hesitate before each answer? This could be a sign that they don't really know their material or are making it up—particularly if the answer turns out to be vague.

Service and More Service

You want a dealer who looks out for your interests, as well as his own. Hopefully, you will find salespeople who are not just trying to sell you something, but are hobbyists who also share your joy for the hobby. You don't want to be sold products that don't work, or items you don't need.

A good dealer will suggest additional products that you need or may find of use—items that you may not have considered—but he won't try to offer you a product for every little problem. Sometimes, there are simpler, cheaper, or even free ways to solve your problems, and your dealer should be willing to volunteer that information.

Besides courteous service, a good dealer will offer additional professional services. Some of these will be freebies, some not. For example, your dealer may offer free water testing. You bring in a sample from your tanks, and they'll do a quick workup for you. (That doesn't mean you shouldn't regularly monitor your water quality on your own.)

Some dealers will offer free repair service on pumps, filters, heaters, and other equipment—charging only for parts. Be aware that you may have to leave the item for repair at their convenience, and you may have to wait for parts to be ordered. Most dealers don't carry much in the way of replacement parts, and their distributors probably only offer them a spotty selection of repair parts.

If your dealer offers free instructional seminars, take advantage of them. Usually they will be on topics suited for beginners, but advanced topics may be covered as well. Sometimes guest speakers who are well-known in the trade may be brought in. It is a great way to learn, have fun, and maybe even make some new friends.

Another service your dealer may offer is aquarium drilling. Yes, most glass can be drilled with the proper tools. More and more people are having holes drilled in their tanks to allow for under-tank plumbing.

Some stores will offer custom-built aquariums and cabinets for sale. These items are more expensive, but are designed to your specifications.

Your dealer also may offer aquarium servicing. In this type of service, you pay your dealer to come to your home and install an aquarium or perform routine maintenance on one. The service may be performed on equipment that you own, or you may lease the aquarium from the dealer. There are many ways this can be done, tailored to each customer. You may even set it up so that the service occasionally swaps fish and decorations in your tank, so you have something new to look at. Most aquarium service companies will ask you to sign a contract that explains your obligations and theirs.

All tropical fish stores offer free advice on treatment of fish diseases. Granted, some are much better at it than others. You may even get lucky and find a store that is willing to do some microscopic examination of your fish when they are sick. This is not very common, though.

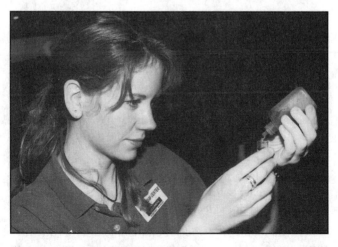

Some dealers offer water-testing services. Here, Alexandra runs a pH test.

Another sign of a good store is the availability of live foods. It is highly entertaining to watch fish feed the way they do in nature. Goldfish, guppies, brine shrimp, and blackworms are the most common live foods, but there are others, and an exceptional dealer will have them available for sale, too.

How Much Is That Fishy in the Window?

It is a Saturday afternoon and you are shopping for aquarium supplies at Super Duper Tropicals, your favorite aquarium store. Today, you happen to be thinking about setting up another aquarium, so you are looking at the various filters that are available. Let's say you find two similar filters, of two different brands. Both are rated at the same number of gallons per hour, are designed for the same size aquariums, but use different types of filter media. One filter is $5 more than the other. Interestingly, the cheaper filter can be bought for $1 less at D&D Tropicals down the street. (By the way, in this story D&D stands for "dead and dying.")

Of the two brands of filters, which is better? Which one will you buy? Since it appears that the dingy store down the street may sell at a lower price than your favorite store, will you go there to buy it?

Every dealer has a different method of pricing his merchandise. So as you shop around, you may find a large range of prices for the same items. Prices will vary from store to store and by geographic region. Welcome to the real world.

Now, everyone loves to get a good deal. None of us wants to pay more for an item than we need to. I hope that you find a good bargain every time you go shopping. But keep this in mind: Price is not everything.

When you look at the price of an item, take a minute to think about what you are getting for your money—it's not just what is inside the package in your hand. In the above example of the two filters, did your dealer take time to explain why one is a much better choice than the other? Did he give you advice on how to set it up? Has he helped you in the past, even when you weren't making a purchase? In my example, I stated that you were making this comparison in your favorite dealer's store. Why is he your favorite dealer?

I'll Tell You Where to Go

There are many places to shop for fish and supplies, and I don't just mean dedicated fish and pet stores. Let's talk about some of these choices, and the advantages and disadvantages of each. I will admit up front that I'm about to stereotype some of these options for you, but my descriptions will be based on what you would commonly find. However, let me emphasize that every seller should be judged individually. There are good ones and bad ones of every type.

Pet Stores

Most of you will be buying your fish and supplies from pet stores. These stores will sell other animals in addition to fish. While a pet store doesn't specialize in fish, the aquarium and fish departments typically count for half the business in a neighborhood pet store. So there is a very good chance that there will be staff on duty who know their stuff when it comes to fish.

Tropical Fish Stores

The best place to buy your aquariums, fish, and supplies is from a dedicated tropical fish store. Unfortunately, there are not many of them out there, except in the larger cities.

The great thing about the dedicated aquarium store is that the people working there are the most likely to know what they're doing. They are there because they like keeping fish. When people like something, they learn about it. So you are most likely to get good advice, find the best equipment, and see the healthiest fish in this store. Count your blessings if you've got one nearby.

Superstores

This is a relatively new category. In the last few years, the pet business has changed a lot. Smaller mom-and-pop stores used to be the norm, but many have disappeared with the appearance of gigantic retail pet superstore chains that have sprung up around the country. These chains move into a market and, due to their size and buying power, run many existing smaller stores out of business with prices that are temporarily lower. The superstore chains have recently started gobbling each other up. At present, they have pretty much whittled themselves down to two major players.

These superstores focus on maintaining an inventory of low-overhead dry goods, particularly dog and cat foods, and carry little in the way of high-maintenance livestock. In other words, they gear their business toward selling supplies, not fish or pets.

What are the advantages and disadvantages? One thing I must give the superstores credit for is that they have brought a degree of professionalism to the pet business. The stores are large, nicely laid out and merchandised, and the selection is good. Since they are actual pet stores and not just pet departments, there is a semi-decent chance that you could find the equipment you need and someone to help you.

However, the odds of that are not as good as they could be, because the stores' emphasis is on dry goods, especially dog and cat food. These stores were designed to be low maintenance, self-serve operations. They have livestock, but no one ever seems to buy any of it.

There are very few dedicated tropical fish superstores around the country, but the ones I've seen have been well worth the trip. It's a lot of fun to walk into a huge store and find upwards of 600 aquariums full of fish to pick from, supplies galore, and wall-to-wall fish geeks.

Mail Order

If you live in a rural area, you may not have an aquarium shop anywhere nearby. You may have no other choice than to order supplies through the mail. There are a few places around the country that sell through the mail, often at very good prices. In fact, I've sometimes seen stuff for sale at prices less than what your dealer pays through his distributor.

Fish and Tips

If you buy mail order, it is majorly uncool to go first to your local dealer and have him spend time educating you on what stuff to buy and how to hook it up, only to turn around and buy it somewhere else. When you find a good dealer, keep him in business by shopping there.

Garage Sales

Aquariums are often offered for sale in the classified ad section of your local newspaper. You will find them in the occasional garage sale, too. Depending on how much you know, you could get a really good deal, or waste a lot of money. It is risky to buy this way.

It's Guaranteed

Sometimes things go wrong. When they do, you may be able to take advantage of a dealer's or manufacturer's warranty. Most dealers offer some type of guarantee on their livestock, and most dry goods will have a manufacturer's warranty.

Warranties are there to protect you from product defects. They don't cover your negligence. Before trying to collect on a guarantee when something goes wrong, you need to consider if the problem really was a defect or if it was due to something done incorrectly on your end.

Fish and Tips

Always open packages carefully and in a way that you can easily reseal them. If you need to return an item because it's the wrong size or style, you won't be able to do so if you shredded the package when you opened it.

For example, if you buy a glass canopy and find that it has a crack when you get home and open the box, your dealer should be happy to replace it. On the other hand, if you buy a glass canopy and accidentally drop it on the floor, you shouldn't expect the dealer or manufacturer to pay for it.

Likewise, a fish that dies of disease or unknown reasons within the warranty period should be readily replaced by your dealer. However, if the fish died because you forgot to cover your tank and it jumped out, or because your ammonia levels are sky high, then it really isn't fair to ask for someone else to pay. The fish has already paid with its life.

Typical Guarantees

Every manufacturer has a different guarantee, and so does every dealer. So there is no way that I can explain this topic fully. However, I can tell you about some typical guarantees. You probably will find similar guarantees at your local shops.

➤ *Aquariums.* Smaller aquariums usually have a 90-day warranty. Larger models may have warranties of one, two, five, or up to 15 years. Occasionally, I've seen tanks offered with lifetime warranties. Be sure to ask for details, because sometimes the extended warranty requires that you buy the manufacturer's aquarium stand at the same time you purchase the tank.

➤ *Dry goods.* Warranties on packaged merchandise will vary by item. Heaters usually have a 90-day or one-year warranty. Air pumps, filters, and lights (the fixture, not the bulb) often have a one-year warranty. Most other items only guarantee that they are not broken when you buy them. It is a good idea to save receipts for your major pieces of equipment, and to save copies of the manufacturer's warranty. Sometimes it is printed on the box, sometimes it is printed on a slip of paper inside. Other times you won't be able to find a warranty printed anywhere.

➤ *Fish and plants.* Check with your dealer for details on his livestock guarantee. Every dealer's guarantee is different. Some give 24 or 48 hours, and some give a full week. Others give no guarantee at all, or guarantee freshwater fish but not saltwater fish. The guarantee may be for full replacement, half-price replacement, or (rarely) full refund.

Something's Fishy

Always inspect your aquarium before you buy it. Chips on corners indicate damage and are weak points where cracks may develop. Reject any aquarium that has chips.

How to Collect

To collect on a fish guarantee, you usually will need three things:

➤ *An identifiable dead body.* It is proof of death, and the dealer needs to see it to identify the species. He'll also take a quick look to see if there were bites taken out of the fish, suggesting that aggression was the cause of demise.

➤ *Your sales receipt.* The sales receipt proves that you are within the time limit of the guarantee and that you didn't buy the fish at another store.

➤ *A water sample from your tank.* Keep it separate from the dead body! Most dealers will want to run a quick test of your water to see if they spot any problems. If they find problems with the water, dealers usually will still guarantee the fish, but will recommend that you take a credit slip instead of a replacement. It would be better to fix the problem before adding more fish.

Here is a quick checklist for you to follow when returning packaged merchandise:

✓ Before exercising a guarantee, review its terms. Be sure you are within the allowable time limit, and be sure it is a defect, not misuse, that caused the problem.

✓ Does the guarantee say to return the item to your dealer or to send it to the manufacturer?

✓ Gather your sales receipt to establish proof of purchase and date of purchase.

✓ Gather the merchandise that you want to return. If you are returning new merchandise that is the wrong size or style, be sure you have the original, undamaged package and any warranty sheets and instruction cards that came inside. Your dealer needs to be able to resell this unused item.

Fish and Tips

When returning merchandise, take your itemized cash register receipt. Unitemized charge card slips won't do.

Chapter 3

Select Your Aquarium, Stand, and Gravel

In This Chapter

➤ Decide between glass and acrylic

➤ Tips for choosing the best size and shape

➤ The difference between starter kits and complete outfits

➤ Choose a proper aquarium stand

➤ Choose your substrate

Aquariums come in many shapes and sizes. You are probably familiar with the typical rectangular aquarium, but did you know there are also pentagonal, hexagonal, spherical, and triangular tanks? Did you know that standard aquariums range in size from one gallon up to 300 gallons? Or that custom-built tanks could go even larger? Before I talk about how to choose specific pieces of equipment, there are some important considerations.

Make Sure It Will Fit

Before buying an aquarium, you should decide where you are going to put it. Take time to measure the space. You don't want your tank to stick out too far into a hallway or block a doorway. Measure how tall the tank and stand together can be. You want to be sure they won't block access to a window or an electrical circuit panel, or bump into overhead shelves or cabinets. Allow a bit extra so there is room to open the lid to maintain the aquarium.

Also measure how wide your tank can be (from front to back). Remember that you may need to leave a bit of space behind it for any hang-on-the-back filters. Minimally, you need to allow enough room for electrical cords, air lines, or filter hoses to run behind the tank. Write down all these measurements and take them with you when you go shopping. That way, you will be able to pick an aquarium and stand that fit into the space you've chosen.

Acrylic May Be Idyllic

When you go shopping for your aquarium, you will need to decide if you want glass or acrylic. Oddly, you may find this decision was made for you, because your dealer will often stock only one or the other. Both types have their advantages and disadvantages, though. So if you want acrylic, and your dealer only stocks glass, either find another dealer or see if you can place a special order.

Many people prefer acrylic tanks. They have a different look than glass tanks, and often it is the look alone that will be the deciding factor. After all, an aquarium with fish is a work of art, and everyone has their own ideas of what it is that constitutes art. Acrylic tanks have a "cleaner" look than glass tanks. That is, acrylic is clearer than glass, and acrylic tanks are usually manufactured using single-piece construction—one sheet of acrylic is heated and bent to form the front and sides of the aquarium. So the corners are seamless, rounded, and completely transparent. Acrylic tanks also have the more modern look of space-age plastics.

One downside is that acrylic is a bit more flexible than glass. So once the tank is full and water presses outward on the sides, the material bows slightly. This happens with glass, too, but it is not as pronounced. Now, don't get me wrong. This bowing is only slight and doesn't pose any strength problems. The disadvantage is that this slight distortion presents more curved surfaces to reflect light from the room. So depending on your room lighting, there may be more curvy reflections to interfere with your viewing.

One advantage of acrylic is that it is lighter than glass. It will take only one or two people to move an empty acrylic aquarium around, whereas it may take up to four to move a glass tank of the same size. Acrylic is also stronger than glass. Yes, it can be cracked or shattered, but it takes quite a bit more force to do it. Also, typical construction involves using solvents to weld the seams together at the molecular level. So an acrylic tank is effectively a one-piece deal with seams that are difficult to split. I would like to add a caveat here: It depends on the manufacturing technique. There are some brands that use thick acrylic glues to bond the panels, instead of the thin liquid solvent. Those tanks aren't as strong.

Acrylic tanks can also be purchased with solid-colored backs—usually blue or black—eliminating the need to buy a separate background. These tanks have colored acrylic rear panels, instead of the typical clear back. Of course, an acrylic background is there to stay, and you can't change to a different color or scene later.

Acrylic tanks have an integral welded top that helps to strengthen the sides of the tank. It is clear, just like the bottom, but has cutouts to allow access for filters, heaters, feeding, and maintenance. So there is no need to buy a separate glass cover. The integral top also prevents much of the mineral build up that you could get at the edge of a glass cover. You can also drill acrylic with typical household tools. So if you want to install plumbing for through-the-wall or through-the-bottom filtration, you can do it yourself.

Something's Fishy

You need to be more careful when scrubbing algae on your acrylic tank. It is not safe to use razor blades on acrylic, and even some algae pads are too rough and can cause damage. Be especially careful not to get bits of gravel between the acrylic and the scrubber pad.

Still, acrylic isn't perfect. It has its disadvantages, too. For starters, acrylic is softer than glass, so it scratches more easily. If you or your fish are prone to knocking large rocks against the sides, you may soon find your tank scratched.

Is Glass First Class?

Personally, I prefer glass tanks. I like the appearance of acrylic better, but I worry about scratching the sides. I've seen many scratched-up acrylic tanks. In fairness, there are kits you can buy to polish out scratches in acrylic, but I find them to be a pain. Some involve liquid polishes for fine scratches and various sizes of abrasive screens for deeper scrapes.

Glass is not as strong as acrylic, but it is plenty strong enough. Glass gives a slightly greenish cast to the aquarium, especially on larger tanks where the glass is thick. However, there has recently been a move toward manufacturing tanks with glass that is more optically clear.

Glass tanks are made by gluing panes together with silicone rubber sealant. Of course, the corners are not transparent because of this, and are not smooth and rounded like acrylic. Rather, glass tanks have sharp angles on the corners—polished, so that you don't get cut on them. Since the corners aren't rounded, you don't get the funhouse mirror distortion that you get on the corners of acrylic tanks.

Glass aquariums come with glued-on plastic frames on the top and bottom. Usually, the frames come in basic black, dark or light woodgrain finishes (referred to as walnut or oak), or a gray granite-type finish. There are other, less common, colors that you may stumble across, as well. The tanks are identical, except for the color of the frames. You typically choose the color that will match your aquarium stand and the decor of your home.

Glass aquariums are usually clear on all four sides, but there are some brands that have solid-colored acrylic backgrounds glued inside. Also, you may occasionally find models with integral mirror backs. These tanks reflect the decorations inside the tank to make it appear twice as deep. Pretty cool, huh? Of course, the downside of a mirror background is that you may see the reflection of a familiar fool looking back at you!

Glass aquariums can sometimes be drilled for through-the-wall plumbing of filters. It depends on the type of glass. I'll talk about that in a moment, but first I want to mention that both glass and acrylic tanks are often available pre-drilled, with plumbing installed, ready to connect to the proper filter. These tanks are commonly referred to as "reef ready" because reef tank hobbyists tend to prefer to put their filters in the cabinet underneath the tank. They can be used for freshwater or saltwater, though.

Shapes and Footprints

Aquariums come in all shapes and sizes. Which shape is best? There are a couple of things to consider. First, an aquarium with flat sides is best. Fortunately, that includes most tank shapes. It really only rules out spheres and those tanks with slanted fronts that have recently hit the market. Rectangles, hexagons, and pentagons are fine. Flat-sided tanks are best because they maximize the surface area of your tank.

Wide, low aquariums are also better than tall, narrow ones. Again, this maximizes the surface area per gallon. As an example, let's take two aquariums. One is 20 inches long by 10 inches wide by 10 inches high. The other is 10 by 10 by 20. Both have the same volume of 2,000 cubic inches (length × width × height). However, the first tank will have a bigger footprint (how much space the tank takes up on a table), providing it with a water surface of 200 square inches (length × width). The second tank will have a water surface of only 100 square inches (length × width), or only half as much!

Both tanks hold the same amount of water, but one has a footprint and surface area that is twice the size of the other. Why is this important? First, oxygen and carbon dioxide exchange at the surface, so the larger the surface area, the better the aeration of the tank. Second, a tank with a larger footprint provides more room for fish to swim—fish prefer swimming back and forth to up and down—and also provides more bottom territory for fish to stake out. In other words, your fish will be more comfortable in the wide, low aquarium than in the tall, narrow one.

This does not mean you can't buy a tall, narrow tank, if that is what you really like. Please feel free. Just buy fewer fish for the tank, and be sure they are members of a less territorial species.

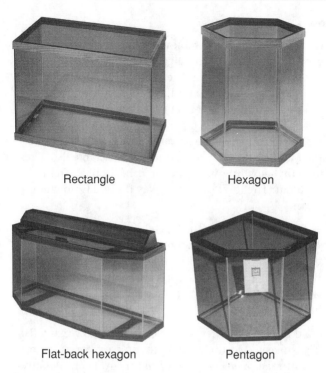

Rectangle   Hexagon

Flat-back hexagon   Pentagon

Some typical aquarium shapes. (Photos courtesy of Perfecto Manufacturing)

Aquariums are sold in standard sizes and dimensions, but the stated size of the tank in gallons is based roughly on external dimensions. To calculate the *true* volume of your aquarium, measure the *inside* length, width, and height (all in inches), multiply them together, and divide by 231 to get gallons. So if a tank had inside dimensions of $30 \times 10 \times 10$, multiplying gives you 3,000. Divide by 231 to get 12.98 gallons. True gallon capacity is almost always less than the capacity stated on the label.

Bigger Is Better

Always buy the biggest tank you can afford that will fit in your designated space. Bigger is better because a big tank provides a more stable environment. It is safer for your fish. A couple of extra flakes of food can pollute a tiny tank, but have no effect on a larger one. A larger tank is less subject to temperature fluctuations. Besides, it takes almost the same amount of time to maintain a small tank as it does a large one. A larger tank also gives more maneuvering space for the fish, should a fight break out. The loser can't get away if there is nowhere to run.

The best reason to buy the biggest tank you can afford is because you will quickly wish that you had more room to keep more species of fish! As a dealer, I hear this lament all the time. You will be surprised at how fast you can fill an aquarium, given all the choices of interesting species that are available.

Avoid mini tanks. They will severely limit how many fish you can keep. Most have room for only one or two fish, *no matter how many are pictured on the box!* I consider anything under 10 gallons to be a mini tank, and most are closer to one or two gallons in size. Some come in novelty shapes, fashioned to look like gum-ball machines, Garfield the Cat, or giant crayons, for example. Others are miniature hexagonal aquariums. Some have no filters, others have the light unnaturally positioned *under* the tank. Sheesh! Anyway, unless your space is severely limited, or you at least have some fishkeeping experience under your belt, please avoid these fish-torturing tanks.

Fish bowls are even worse. They come in sizes even smaller than mini tanks and rarely include filters. If each inch of fish should have one gallon of *filtered* water, how many one-inch fish do you think you can safely fit in an *unfiltered* one-quart fish bowl?

If you are thinking you would rather start out small to see how things work out, and then move up to something larger, consider that your chances of success are much lower with a small aquarium. It's better to get the big tank and enjoy it than to get a mini tank that will end up collecting dust in the attic.

Starter Kits vs. Complete Outfits

Often the easiest way to get started is to buy one of the complete kits that your dealer offers. They often include a break on the price. But before we talk in detail about what such a kit would include, let me define my terminology. I define a "complete" aquarium kit as one that includes everything you need to set up the tank—except your choices of decorations and livestock. Those items will need to be purchased separately. A "starter" kit is anything less than that.

Unfortunately, you will often see starter kits labeled as complete kits, although they are missing many necessary items. Now, don't get me wrong. There is nothing wrong with buying a starter kit, if you know what other items you need to buy and actually do buy them. It's just that I've seen too many consumers buy kits that they thought were complete, only to learn (often the hard way) that they need to buy more stuff. This problem is more frequent with kits purchased somewhere besides a dedicated aquarium or pet store, though it does happen there, too.

Something's Fishy

You will not find complete aquarium kits for $19.99 or even $29.99. Cheap setups are going to be incomplete and contain inferior items. The equipment needed to properly set up a 10-gallon tank probably will cost you somewhere between $75 and $100, without a stand. I've seen people kill off $100 worth of fish trying to save $20 by buying inferior equipment!

Here is a shopping list of items that I believe make up a *really* complete aquarium kit:

- ➤ Aquarium
- ➤ Full hood with light
- ➤ Filter system
- ➤ Heater
- ➤ Thermometer
- ➤ Gravel
- ➤ Gravel vacuum
- ➤ Food
- ➤ Net
- ➤ Water conditioner
- ➤ pH, ammonia, and nitrite test kits
- ➤ Beginner's book *(this one!)*
- ➤ Aquarium stand

If your budget is tight, you could get the gravel vacuum later. You won't need it for a few weeks, anyway. If your dealer provides a free water-testing service, you may be able to skip the test kits, as well—although I don't recommend doing so. Also, if you have a counter or shelf strong enough to hold your aquarium, you may not need the aquarium stand at all. For those of you who need a stand, read on.

Taking a Stand

Your aquarium stand *must* be strong, flat, and level. Remembering that a full aquarium will weigh around 10 pounds per gallon, you can see that this may be no easy task. While people often do put aquariums on shelves, tables, and countertops, these items are usually not designed to hold that kind of weight. If the stand wobbles or twists, your tank will break.

Usually your best bet is to buy a commercial aquarium stand. Fortunately, there are many styles of them available, all designed to match the finishes on the various styles of aquariums that your dealer sells. They'll also fit well with your household decor.

Fish and Tips

Modern aquariums rest on their bottom plastic frames. So they don't touch the stand in the center, but only around the perimeter. Because of this, you may find stands that are open on top, with no central support. The stands are perfectly fine, and come in handy if you ever want to plumb through the bottom of the tank or see what is hiding under your undergravel filter.

Gravel: Let's Get to the Bottom of It

The first decoration to go into your tank will be the aquarium gravel. You will find that your dealer carries gravel in a wide variety of colors, of varying pebble size. Your first impulse will be to pick your favorite color, or perhaps a color that you think best matches the room. However, that may not be the best way to go.

Once you install your plants and other decorations, the gravel may not be that noticeable. So the appeal of the color, or the way it matches your room, may not even be important. Before choosing a color that you like most, you also should consider how well your fish will like the color. After all, they are the ones who will really be living with it.

Most fish will look better in tanks with dark gravel. I find that black, dark blue, dark green, and dark natural gravels tend to show fish pretty well. White, yellow, pink, and lighter natural gravels may cause the fishes' colors to fade. How much they fade will depend on the species and how many other decorations (plants, rocks, backgrounds, and so forth) are dark colored.

You also need to choose the size of the stones in your gravel mix. Particle sizes ranging from sand to two-inch pebbles can be found in stores. Most aquarium gravel, though, will range from one-eighth inch to one-half inch in diameter.

One-eighth- to one-quarter-inch stones are best. If the particles are too small, they can compact and make it difficult for plants to grow. Small sand-sized particles also can sift through the slots in an undergravel filter plate, if you have one, and clog it up. If the pebbles are too large, then the space between them also becomes larger. This means food can fall down between the stones, where it is out of reach of the fish, and can pollute the tank. If the spaces are large enough, small fish could even get stuck.

Another reason not to pick pebbles of too large a size is that pebble size affects your biological filtration. Smaller stones have more surface area per pound, providing more space to grow helpful bacteria. To illustrate this, think of an apple as representing a large stone. You have a certain amount of surface area, as represented by the red skin of the apple. Now, if you take that apple and cut it in half, you will still have the original surface area *plus* the additional surface area of the two white faces that the cut created.

Gravel in Depth

How much gravel will you need? Well, that depends. You can get away with less gravel, if you just want to cover the bottom. However, if you want to have enough to root your plants, or allow the fish to dig a little without exposing the glass bottom, or to make an undergravel filter function properly, then you should create a layer of gravel that is one and a half to two inches deep. Serious aquatic plant enthusiasts go even deeper, putting three to six inches of gravel in their tanks.

Gravel is usually sold in five-pound, 25-pound, or 50-pound bags. It can be difficult to determine how many pounds of gravel will be right for your tank. One rule I find that works pretty well is to use at least 10 pounds per square foot of bottom. This is a better guideline, because it considers the actual space that you need to fill. There are three standard sizes of 20-gallon tanks on the market, and they have bottoms that are 2.0, 2.5, and 1.4 square feet, respectively. You can see that using a pounds-per-gallon rule to choose your gravel will give quite different results for each of these 20-gallon tanks.

The following table shows how much gravel I recommend for typical sizes of aquariums to achieve a depth of one and a half to two inches. If I list a range, the first number fits the 10-pounds-per-square-foot rule, and the second number is the amount I prefer to recommend—because I feel that the higher number gives an effect more pleasing to the eye. (Some tanks have deeper frames, so the gravel appears to be more shallow. The higher amount of gravel counteracts that.)

Gravel Recommendations

Tank Size (in Gallons)	Tank Footprint (in Inches)	Gravel Needed (in Pounds)
5.5	16 × 8	10
10	20 × 10	15
15	24 × 12	20–25
20XH	20 × 10	15
20H	24 × 12	20–25
20L	30 × 12	25–30
29	30 × 12	25–30
30	36 × 12	30–40
40	48 × 13	45–60
50	36 × 18	45–60
55	48 × 13	45–60

Chapter 4

Choosing Your Filter System

In This Chapter

➤ Learn the basics of filtration

➤ Decide which style of filter is right for you

➤ Explore air pumps and connectors

➤ Examine optional powerheads

Your filter system acts like the internal organs of your aquarium. It functions like the heart, lungs, liver, kidneys, and intestinal tract of your tank. It is thanks to filtration that we are able to keep fish in such small spaces. Without filtration, you would have to greatly reduce the number of fish you keep in your aquarium. You would also have to increase the frequency of water changes.

Your filter is your aquarium's best friend. Don't forget, though, that filters are equipment. They need to have regular maintenance or they will fail to function. Your filter helps clean the tank, but *you* have to clean the filter. I will talk about that more in Chapter 12.

Also, don't even begin to think that your filter can remove all types of waste. It can't! There are many dissolved wastes that will only be removed by keeping up with your regular partial water changes. Additionally, those water changes help replenish lost trace elements. Filters do not eliminate the need for water changes.

The Basics of Filtration

There are many brands and styles of filters, and they work in many ways. It may take one or more to do the job satisfactorily. There are three basic types of filtration that your filter system needs to provide:

> ➤ Mechanical filtration

> ➤ Biological filtration

> ➤ Chemical filtration

Mechanical Filtration

Mechanical filtration is what the typical person thinks of when they think of filtration. With a mechanical filter, particles of solid waste are physically removed by passing the water through filter media. Most types of filters provide some degree of mechanical filtration. Undergravel filters collect debris that has settled in the gravel. Most other filters collect debris in removable or disposable filter media.

Biological Filtration

Bio-filtration is probably the most important type of filtration. It works by using helpful bacteria to break down fish waste, particularly ammonia, that the fish excrete. Be sure to read Chapter 10 for details on cycling your new tank.

All filters provide some biological filtration, but some are better at it than others. Two things determine how well a filter performs this function. First, the more filter area there is, the better. That is because the helpful bacteria live on all the solid surfaces in the tank. The more surface area provided by your filter media, the more room there is for these bacteria to colonize.

Second, disposable filter media affect biological filtration. Disposable media are less preferable than media that can be rinsed and reused. You see, every time you throw away your filter media, you throw away all the helpful bacteria living on it, too. So the new medium must be re-colonized with helpful bacteria before it works at maximum efficiency.

Chemical Filtration

Chemical filtration means using a chemical compound to collect certain types of dissolved waste. In addition, chemical filtration helps keep the water clear. Without the use of activated carbon, your water may be quite transparent but may develop a yellow cast from the buildup of dissolved organic materials.

Granular activated carbon (GAC) is the most common chemical filter medium used, but there are also various resinous beads used to soften water and to remove copper, phosphates, organics, and other metabolites. Also, zeolite (ammo-chips) is sometimes used to remove ammonia, nitrates, and phosphates.

The chemical filter media are almost always disposable. That is, after some use, it will no longer be able to adsorb the impurities that you want to remove. In fact, if it becomes fully loaded with waste and your pH changes, the chemical filter medium could release some nasties back into the aquarium. So always change your chemical filter medium on schedule. I recommend that you replace activated carbon monthly. Zeolite and resinous beads (some are rechargeable) should be recharged or replaced monthly. Follow the manufacturer's instructions.

Something's Fishy

Activated carbon is not rechargeable. You may hear
people say that you can recharge it by baking it in an
oven. However, that is not true—not unless you have a
special super-hot, low-oxygen oven. (You don't!) After a
month, throw away the old carbon and buy new.

Some chemical filtration products on the market that to
be good for up to six months. While these are excellent
products, you should never try to stretch their useful lives
to that point, unless you have an unusually low bioload.
Rather, replace these products every month or so.

Sifting Through the Choices

Your dealer probably will offer a perplexing array of filters
in many brands, shapes, and sizes. Don't be afraid to ask for
his advice in picking the right filter or filters for your tank.

When purchasing filters, first compare features. Then
compare prices. Be sure to factor in the regular cost of any
replacement filter media that may be needed. Sometimes
cheaper filters use more expensive media and end up being more costly in the long run.

All filters should be installed as designed. Do not waste
your time trying to hybridize them to make them better.
Doing so could result in disaster. For example, do not try
to replace the overflow system on a trickle filter with a
siphon, or try to plumb a canister filter to run more than
one tank. If you do, the result *will* be a flood or a burned
out pump. Or both!

Undergravel Filters

For many years these were the most popular choice, and still are for many people. The good feature of undergravel filters is that you don't have to replace any filter media, so they are very cheap to operate. Rather, use a gravel vacuum to siphon debris out of the gravel when you do your partial water changes.

Undergravel filters work on a simple principle. The filter consists of a perforated platform that sits under the gravel in your tank. Rising from the filter are one or more lift-tubes. These days, they are usually one-inch diameter tubes, and they have an air line with a small air diffuser hanging inside. Outside the tank is an air pump that drives the filter.

Air is pumped down the center of the filter lift-tube(s), and as the bubbles rise from the bottom, they push water ahead of them. The effect is that water gets pulled down through the gravel, pulled through the slots in the filter plate, and then pulled from under the platform and pushed up the lift-tube back into the tank, where the cycle begins again.

As the water is pulled through the gravel, debris gets trapped between the stones (mechanical filtration). Also, helpful bacteria living on every particle of gravel will break down ammonia that is excreted by the fish (bio-filtration). Some models have small activated-carbon cartridges atop the lift-tubes. These provide minimal chemical filtration.

I think undergravel filters are great for most tanks. You must remember, though, that the gravel is the filter medium. Like all filters, you must clean the medium regularly, or it will become too clogged to function. If you keep up your regular partial water changes and use a gravel vacuum, the undergravel filter may be the only filter system you need. However, it also helps to add a small outside power filter to provide additional chemical filtration.

Pick gravel that has the correct particle size. One-eighth-to one-quarter-inch diameter particles are good. If the particles are too large, the spaces between them will be too large to trap debris. Worse, the spaces would be large enough to let food fall into the gravel and become trapped, where it can't be reached by the fish. Do not use sand, as it will sift down through the filter plate and clog the filter.

You'll also need the right amount of gravel. Gravel is the filter medium in this system. Use a one-and-a-half- to two-inch-deep layer. If the gravel isn't deep enough, it will have a very hard time trapping debris.

There are some situations where undergravel filters aren't a good choice. One situation would be in a tank that has large piles of rocks, such as an African cichlid tank. In this setup, you will be unable to perform proper maintenance because the rocks will impede use of your gravel vacuum. Additionally, some species, including African cichlids, like to dig a lot. If they dig and expose the filter plate, the filter won't function fully. You see, water takes the path of least resistance. So if slots in the filter plate become uncovered, water will tend to take that path, rather than filtering down through the gravel where the filtration takes place. Also, digging fish will keep stirring the trapped debris out of the filter bed.

Finally, instead of an air pump, a powerhead may be used to run an undergravel filter. I will tell you about powerheads and air pumps shortly.

Outside Power Filters

These motorized plastic boxes hang on the back of your aquarium. Changeable filter media go inside the box. An intake tube hangs into the tank, and the motor draws water directly up through it. The water then flows through

A typical undergravel filter (left) and an outside power filter.

the media, where mechanical, biological, and chemical filtration all take place. The water is then typically returned to the aquarium via a waterfall chute. Since there is a built-in motor, no additional pumps are required.

Outside power filters are great and provide all three types of filtration. Some are a little better than others, though. I recommend the models that use a sponge as one type of filter medium. The sponge collects debris, but also provides a place for helpful bacteria to colonize. When it gets dirty, you rinse it out and reuse it, retaining many of your helpful bacteria. Other models use disposable cartridges made up of a sandwich of polyester filter media and activated carbon.

Some recent versions include something called a Bio-Wheel. This is a paddle-boat-like wheel suspended above the filter box. As water flows through, it rotates the wheel, alternately wetting it and exposing it to the air. Helpful bacteria grow on the wheel. Since there is 30,000 times as much oxygen in air as there is in water, and since these bacteria require oxygen to break down waste, they are quite efficient in this setup.

Fish and Tips

When buying an outside power filter, be sure to follow the recommendations of your dealer. Not only do you need to choose a model that is adequate for the size of your tank, but you need to be sure you get one that will fit the frame of your brand of aquarium. Some tanks have thicker frames, requiring a slightly larger filter.

Canister Filters

Over the years, these have become my favorite filters because they are so versatile. Canister filters resemble miniature Wet-Vacs, and can provide all three types of filtration—mechanical, biological, and chemical. There is a canister that sits underneath your aquarium and connects to the tank via input and output hoses. Inside are various styles of filter media. The built-in motor pumps the water through the filter.

These filters are great for tanks with lots of plants, rocks, or other decorations. With an outside power filter, you have no choice where the output will be. With canister filters, you can install the output hose so that it pumps the water where you want it, and you can even T it off so that it pumps to more than one location (in the same aquarium). The output can be set up to spray the water back in a single large jet, or through a perforated spray bar that has many small jets.

The brands I like best use three types of filter media, and have separate inner compartments for them. Typically, the first compartment will contain ceramic noodles. These evenly channel the water flow, trap larger particles of debris, and provide space for helpful bacteria to colonize. The second chamber will be used for activated carbon or other chemical filter media, and the third chamber contains a sponge. The chemical filter media is the only media that you replace. When dirty, the ceramic noodles and sponge are rinsed and reused, retaining helpful bacteria. Other brands of canister filters use polyester sleeves, pleated cartridges, and other types of filter media.

Something's Fishy

If you buy a canister filter, be sure your model comes with shut-off valves for each hose, or you could have water back-siphoning onto your carpet when you disconnect the filter for cleaning.

One other consideration with canister filters is that some are easier to change than others. You may want to ask your dealer's advice on this topic.

Box or Corner Filters

This is the oldest style of filter. It consists of a small plastic box into which you put polyester filter floss and activated carbon. An air pump drives water through the device. While box filters do have their uses, they are ugly, have limited capacity, and really aren't the best choice. They do provide all three types of filtration, though. You may commonly find box filters in cheap starter kits, to keep the price low.

Internal Cartridge Filters

There are a couple styles of internal cartridge filters. None are good choices. One is a cross between a box filter and an outside power filter. Its shape is more like a box filter, and it is also powered by an air pump, but it uses a filter cartridge similar to those in outside power filters. It provides low levels of all three types of filtration.

The other type of cartridge filter is merely a replaceable slotted cartridge with chemical filter media inside. It is designed to be used as a supplementary filter in small tanks.

Sponge Filters

These also have limited use in most tanks. I love to use them in quarantine and fry tanks, though. They do a very good job of biological filtration, and they don't trap baby fish the way all other filters do. They are not very good at collecting debris, however. Also, they go inside the tank, so they are ugly to look at. There are models that stick to the side with suction cups, and models that rest on the bottom. You need a small air pump to drive this filter. They don't do chemical filtration.

Air Pumps

Air pumps are mainly used to drive various types of filters. But they can also be used to power decorative airstones and ornaments. Air pumps come in many sizes, which include not only varying degrees of power, but varying numbers of outlets. Air pumps go *outside* the tank. Putting them under water can destroy them and electrocute you.

Fish School

An *airstone* is usually an artificial rock that is porous enough to allow air to pass through it, thus splitting the airstream into tiny bubbles.

You must pick the right size pump for the job, and this can be difficult because the packaging will often say "good for tanks up to X number of gallons." That information is fairly useless, because you should not pick your air pump based on the size of your tank. Instead, you should pick it based on what you want it to run. For example, it would take a large air pump to run the four outlets on the undergravel filter of a 55-gallon tank. But it would take a very small air pump to place one of those bubbling treasure chests in the very same tank.

So choose your air pump based on your needs, not the tank size. Your dealer should be able to advise you regarding the various brands and models.

Most air pumps available for fish tanks are diaphragm pumps. That is, they have a plunger-shaped rubber diaphragm that vibrates 60 times per second, pumping air. As the diaphragms age and wear, they may crack. There are other parts, including rubber valve flappers, that may wear or get dirty and clogged. Your dealer sells repair kits for when this happens, and may even offer repair services.

Fish and Tips

If you find your air pump only works in shallow water but not when you put the air line to the bottom of the tank, your pump has a cracked diaphragm. Your dealer sells replacement parts.

The best way to extend the life of your air pump is to make sure your airstones or filter outlets aren't clogged. Back-pressure from clogged outlets is the chief cause of wear on diaphragms. The built-up pressure is what stretches and cracks them.

You will need an air line to go with your air pump, and may also need gang-valves to increase the number of outlets you can run. We'll talk more about those items in Chapter 6 on choosing supplies.

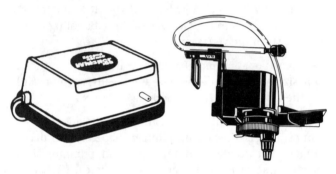

Air pumps (left) and powerheads can be used to power undergravel filters.

Powerheads

Powerheads are small water pumps that can be used to power an undergravel filter, instead of using an air pump. The powerhead sits on top of the undergravel filter lift-tube and draws water directly. It has an adjustment that lets you control the flow to some extent, and an adjustment that lets you draw outside air into the mix.

Some people like powerheads. Some like air pumps. I honestly can't say that one has real advantages over the other. They do the same job.

You can also use powerheads for stand-alone circulation. They can be suction-cupped to the inside glass, or clamped to the tank frame, and you direct the flow where you want it. So some people use them in addition to their filter systems to provide extra current.

Chapter 5

Hot Picks in Heating and Lighting

In This Chapter

➤ How to choose the right heater for your tank

➤ Ways to prevent broken heater tubes

➤ Learn how your heater's thermostat works

➤ Determine your lighting needs

➤ Learn about incandescent and fluorescent lighting

➤ Examine the relative advantages of glass canopies and full-hoods

Most of the fish we keep in aquariums are tropical fish. That means they come from warm climates. To keep them comfortable and healthy, we need to be sure their aquariums are warm enough. In other words, most of us will need to purchase aquarium heaters for our tanks.

Most tropical fish prefer to be kept at 75° to 78°F (24° to 26°C). But even if you keep cold-water fish, it can be a good idea to have an aquarium heater. It's possible for a winter cold snap to drop temperatures below ideal levels. Even Florida gets freezing weather, sometimes. Further, if the furnace in your house malfunctions, an aquarium heater may be the only salvation for your fish.

Heating Systems

Aquarium heaters have built-in thermostats which, when properly set, will turn the heater on only when needed. So it should be safe to set the heater and feel secure that it will automatically kick on if required.

To find a good selection of aquarium heaters, you simply need to visit your local pet store. Your dealer will be able to hook you up with the proper size and style of heater to fit your tank and your budget.

Many things can influence your choice of aquarium heaters. Your budget may be the first thing. Aquarium heaters come in quite a range of prices. The hang-on-the-tank versions are usually cheaper. Fully submersible models will cost more. Like most merchandise, the various brands and models will come with different features. Some features will affect the price.

Clip-On vs. Submersible

Is a submersible heater better than a hang-on-the-tank one? Usually, either style will do the job quite well. However, there are situations where one choice is better than the other. If you are on a limited budget, the hang-on-the-tank heater probably will be your only choice. Submersible heaters have some additional features that you may need or want if you can afford one.

Submersible heaters are fully submersible (of course!). That means you can place the entire heater under water, including parts of the cord. One good thing about this is that you can hide the heater behind some driftwood or rocks and hardly be aware that it is there. Don't hide the pilot light, though. You won't be able to tell if the heater is functioning! Submersible heaters come with suction cups that mount them to the side glass. Both vertical and horizontal mounting are possible.

Heater Styles

To help you choose between clip-on and submersible, let's look at the many styles available of both types. I'll start with the cheapest models and work up.

Mini-Tank Heater

You may run across dealers selling this small seven-watt submersible heater for tiny tanks. It is only six inches long and has no thermostat. So when you plug it in, it turns on and stays on. It is not a full-fledged automatic heating system. Rather, its purpose is to be a "better than nothing" alternative. However, it could be worse than nothing! Since it doesn't shut off, there are situations where it could provide too much heat for the job.

Economy Heater

These are the typical, inexpensive clip-on heaters that come with most aquarium kits. Economy heaters are best-sellers because they are the cheapest. However, they are not the most dependable. Also, the thermostats are more prone to cause static interference on your radio. Most companies only make these in 25- to 100-watt sizes, and they only mount vertically. Typical prices are in the $5 to $10 range.

Deluxe Heater

This hang-on-the-tank heater looks physically very much like an economy heater. However, it has better circuitry or magnetic thermostats, to reduce the possibility of radio interference. It may be available in a larger range of sizes, too. The typical price is around $20.

Submersible Heater

With this model the controls are encased in rubber, so the heater can go completely under water. Older styles of submersible heaters came with thermostats similar to deluxe heaters. In the last few years, models with built-in temperature adjustment scales have become available. If you want to keep your tank at 78°F (26°C), you merely dial it with the control knob. Submersibles usually run $20 and up.

Electronic Heater

These are the top-of-the-line heaters. Unfortunately, you won't find these heaters in many shops because they are fairly expensive—often in the $50 range. Electronic heaters have no moving parts in the thermostat, so they are the most dependable. Often, the thermostat mounts separately from the heater tube, giving more accurate readings.

Watts Hot?

Heaters come in several lengths, typically six inches, eight inches, 10 inches, 12 inches, and 15 inches. With heaters that hang down into the aquarium, be sure not to get a heater that is too long. The heater must usually be at least two inches shorter than the height of your tank. Three or four inches shorter than the tank height is even better. That allows plenty of room for gravel and rocks at the bottom of the tank.

Follow the same rule for submersible heaters, if you are planning to mount them vertically. If you plan to use a horizontal orientation, though, the length of the tank (rather than the depth) will limit the length of the heater.

Aquarium heaters come in several standard sizes of output. Sizes are based on the number of watts they consume when running. Standard wattages are 25w, 50w, 75w, 100w, 150w, 200w, 250w, and 300w, but all wattages aren't available in all brands. Additionally, anything over 200 watts is available only in submersible models.

The Right Size for the Job

Some recent research produced the following two tables.
They give pretty accurate estimates of appropriate heater
sizes. To use the first table, find the size of your tank in
the top row. Then follow the column down until you find
the number of degrees above room temperature that your
tank may need to be heated. For example, if you want a
78°F temperature and your room temperature is only 65°F,
then you need to achieve 13°F of additional heat. When
you find the appropriate figure, look at the wattage in the
far left column to determine what size heater you need.

Wattage Needed to Increase Water Temperature Above Room Temperature

	Aquarium Size, in Gallons				
Heater Watts	**10**	**20**	**29**	**55**	**60**
50	16°F	12°F	10°F		
75	19°F	17°F	15°F		
100	26°F	22°F	19°F	13°F	12°F
150	24°F	22°F	18°F	18°F	
200	30°F	24°F	20°F		
250	32°F	30°F	27°F		
300	38°F	34°F	29°F		

Table courtesy of Aquarium Systems, Inc., makers of Visitherm aquarium heaters.

There's another way to think about this. To use the next
table, find your tank size at the top. Then, read down the
column to see what size heater you need, based on the desired increase above room temperature, as listed on the left.

Heater Selection Guide

Desired Increase in Room Temp.	Aquarium Size, in Gallons							
	5	**10**	**20**	**25**	**40**	**50**	**65**	**75**
9°F	25w	50w	50w	75w	100w	150w	200w	250w
18°F	25w	50w	75w	100w	150w	200w	250w	300w
27°F	75w	100w	150w	200w	300w	400w	500w	600w

Heaters are listed in watts.

Table courtesy of Aquarium Systems, Inc., makers of Visitherm aquarium heaters.

Preventing Breakage

Aquarium heaters are electrical parts sealed within a glass tube. As you know, water and electricity don't mix safely, so be careful not to break your aquarium heater. First, *never take the heater out of the water or put it into water when it's plugged in.* Heaters get red hot when they are on. You can get burned. You can start a fire. Also, if you take a hot heater and put it into cold water, the glass on the heater tube will crack, getting water inside and potentially causing a shock to you or your fish.

Fish and Tips

An aquarium heater cannot function properly if there is no water circulating past it to distribute the heat. Your tank must have aeration or filtration for the heater to work. Without circulation, the water next to the heater will be heated, and the thermostat will sense this and shut off before the rest of the tank gets heat, too.

The second step you need to take will help prevent accidents based on some of the dumb things your fish might do. Many large fish are very good at abusing aquarium heaters. They can bang them against the glass. They can slap them with their tails. I've even known fish that got so severely ticked off at the heater's pilot light blinking at them that they decided to give it a good bite!

To help prevent your fish from breaking the heater, I highly recommend that you install it with suction cups. These will anchor it firmly to the side of the tank so it can't get smacked up against the glass. Submersible heaters usually come with suction cups, but hang-on-the-tank heaters don't. You should buy optional suction cups for those. When you mount your aquarium heater, be sure not to position the suction cups over the heating coils. The suction cups are plastic, and will melt.

Shopping for Thermometers

Every aquarium must have a thermometer. There are no exceptions. How else are you going to know the temperature of your tank? Even if you have a heater with a temperature-control gauge, without a thermometer you will have no way to tell if the heater if functioning properly.

Your dealer sells several varieties of thermometers. All are quite inexpensive. Here are some typical types:

➤ *Floating thermometer.* This is a glass thermometer that floats. If you press it into a front corner of your tank, it will stay there for easy reading. Otherwise, the water current will carry it where it may, and you'll have trouble finding and reading it.

➤ *Standing thermometer.* This is like a floating thermometer, but with extra weight at one end. It sinks to the bottom. You could just drop it in the tank, but I prefer to wedge it in the gravel. Otherwise, the fish tend to knock it around, and it always seems to end up facing backwards in some far corner when you want to see it.

➤ *Stainless steel thermometer.* This is a glass thermometer attached to a metal bracket that hangs over the edge of your tank. I don't much like these because the hanger interferes with the proper nesting of your glass canopy or full hood on top of the tank.

➤ *Liquid crystal thermometer.* You can find this in many shapes, styles, and temperature ranges. It is absolutely the most accurate and easiest to read. It is inexpensive, too. You may note that every liquid crystal thermometer at the store gives the same reading, while the cheaper glass thermometers vary by several degrees. A liquid crystal thermometer mounts on the outside glass. They come in various styles, but my favorite is the horizontal strip version. I like to mount it on the front of the tank, just below the gravel line. It gives a good, accurate reading there, without obstructing my view of the fish. The one disadvantage is that you really should not move it, once installed.

Lighting Systems

Light is very important to your aquarium. Obviously, the primary advantage of having a light on your tank is that it helps you to see the fish. It serves other functions, too. If you have live plants, they need light to sustain themselves. Fish need light, too. Light helps them see and find food. It also helps them to see you coming with the fish food can. It helps them find partners for spawning, or spot predators that are nearby.

Light has some less obvious purposes, too. Regulating circadian rhythm is a primary one—circadian rhythm is the day-night cycle that is regulated by an animal's inner biological clock. Lighting cycles help a fish decide when it is time to eat or rest, and when to breed. Some fish spawn at daybreak, some at night, and so forth. The length of the lighted day, the indoor equivalent of seasons, also affects breeding and other fish behavior.

Sometimes light has some unexpected effects. The typical silver angelfish is a silver fish with vertical black stripes. A dusky angelfish is a solid grayish silver, with no stripes. You may think these are two different varieties of fish, bred for their different appearance, but you'd be wrong. They are the same fish! The colors were determined after birth. The striped fish was raised with a normal day-night cycle. The solid colored fish was raised in 24 hours of light.

Do not leave your light on 24 hours a day. Fish need rest, too, and I am sure you can imagine how hard it would be to get some rest when it is eternally light and you have no eyelids to close. You can buy inexpensive automatic timers to turn your aquarium's light on and off at the same time every day.

How Much Light Is Right?

Obviously, a tank with plastic plants can prosper with a lot less light than a tank with live plants, because plastic plants don't need light to live and grow. In fact, if you are going to use plastic plants only, you don't want strong light because it will tend to cause algae problems.

Some species of live plants, particularly the red ones, need a lot more light to prosper. If you want to get lush plant growth with all species and have more choices of species that you can successfully keep, then you need more light.

So, how much light is right? Well, if you are not going the live plant route, then the typical full-hood or single strip light will provide enough lighting for you to see the fish and enjoy the tank. However, if you want lush plant growth, that will not be enough.

To do well with plants, a common recommendation is to have two to five watts of full-spectrum lighting per gallon of aquarium water. Since I have devoted all of Chapter 14 to planted aquariums, I will save the detailed discussion of the lighting requirements of plants until then (I'll bet you can't wait!).

Bright Choices in Light Bulbs

Before discussing the various types of lighting equipment your dealer may have, I want to talk a bit about the bulbs themselves. The light unit you purchase will house the bulbs, but the bulbs produce the light. It can be difficult choosing because there is a large array of styles varying in color, intensity, and consumption of electricity.

Incandescent Bulbs

These are the bulbs with a screw-in base that fit standard household sockets. The major difference in the aquarium version is the shape. They are elongated, rather than bulbous. Think banana, not pear. *Showcase bulb* is another name for this shape of incandescent lamp. Incandescent bulbs are falling out of style in aquarium setups, and are only available for the smaller tanks.

Most incandescent bulbs put out a white light, with a slightly yellowish cast. There are Gro-Lux style incandescent bulbs that are designed to be better for plant growth. The bulb looks bluish when turned off, but gives off white light with a pinkish cast when lit. I like these better than the standard clear incandescent bulbs because they show the colors of the fish a bit better. Red fish look red under this bulb, whereas they look a bit more orange under the clear bulb. Do not buy colored bulbs (red, yellow, green, blue, pink). They are detrimental to the health of your tank.

Typical sizes for incandescent bulbs are 15 watts for 10-gallon tanks and smaller, and 25 watts for larger units.

Occasionally, you will see 40-watt bulbs available, but be careful using them—the added heat output may melt the plastic housing of your light unit.

Fluorescent Bulbs

These bulbs are similar to ceiling lights that you see in commercial establishments. They are composed of a long tube with pins at each end.

Fluorescent bulbs come in standard lengths and wattages. The diameters of the bulbs do vary a bit, with 1-inch diameter and 1.5-inch diameter bulbs being the norm. Don't concern yourself with the diameter of the bulb, though. They are interchangeable. Just make sure you get the right length and wattage. Particularly, pay attention to the wattage because all bulbs of the same wattage will be the same length.

Fish and Tips

Even though fluorescent bulbs from the hardware store will fit your aquarium's light fixtures, you should buy bulbs from a pet store. The bulbs sold in hardware stores will be of a different spectrum, and may cause algae problems for you.

Fluorescent lighting is a very cost-effective way to light your aquarium. It gives a bright, even flood of light, and uses little electricity. Fluorescent bulbs come in many spectra, but I'll discuss that shortly.

Compact Fluorescent Bulbs

These lights work on the same principle as the fluorescent tubes I just described. However, the bulb has a U-shape and higher output. You can fit more light into a smaller space with compact fluorescents, but they cost more than standard fluorescents. They put out light with an intensity similar to that of VHO tubes, but are cooler and more energy efficient. This style of lighting is becoming more popular in deluxe setups.

A Spectrum of Lighting Choices

Lights come in all colors, but your aquarium will look its best and your fish will stay healthiest under white light. You probably remember from science class that white light is composed of all the colors of the rainbow mixed together. White light is composed of the entire visible spectrum of light.

Sunlight is also composed of all the colors of the rainbow, but also thrown in are colors that are invisible to you and me—infrared (IR) and ultraviolet (UV) wavelengths. Infrared light is heat, and all light bulbs produce heat, but most don't produce ultraviolet wavelengths in any appreciable amounts. This is probably a good thing, because some types of UV light cause sunburns.

However, some ultraviolet light can be helpful. Many animals require it to manufacture their own vitamin D. Humans are such animals. Anyway, light bulbs that give off the full spectrum of visible light, plus small amounts of UV light, are called "full-spectrum" lights. These cost a bit more, but generally produce lighting that is more pleasing to the eye and more healthy for the fish and plants.

Light bulbs are available in a wide array of spectra. Although I've avoided using brand names in this book, I could not find an easy way to describe the spectra of various bulbs without making it so general as to become confusing. So, I am going to present you with a list of bulbs that are available from one popular manufacturer. There are many equivalent brands out there, but this one probably has the widest distribution. You probably won't have trouble finding these, but don't feel that I am recommending this brand above all others. And, don't worry—I wouldn't list them at all if they weren't good bulbs.

Something's Fishy

Colored incandescent bulbs (red, blue, green, yellow, pink) are sometimes sold in pet stores. Do not buy these bulbs! Colored light has been shown to be harmful to fish and other organisms. And ultra-violet light (also called black light) will kill your fish.

The following fluorescent light tubes, from Rolf C. Hagen Corp., are available in most pet stores:

➤ *Aqua-Glo.* This is the version of the Gro-Lux bulb sold for aquariums. When you buy inexpensive fluorescent lamps at an aquarium store, this type of bulb is probably what you will get. It is also style of bulb commonly included with fluorescent hoods. The light is pleasingly white, with a slightly pinkish cast that accents the colors of the fish. Particularly, red fish will look red, rather than orange.

➤ *Sun-Glo.* This is a full-spectrum bulb. The light is white, but with a slight greenish tint that makes plants look superb. It's the color of sunlight on a warm day. Red fish look slightly orange under it, though.

➤ *Power-Glo.* This bulb has a higher intensity than most fluorescent bulbs, but it is not HO or VHO. Some extra blue is mixed into the spectrum, making it good for saltwater corals and freshwater plants. A nice, bright white light.

➤ *Life-Glo*. Similar to the Power-Glo bulb, but it has an internal reflector that directs the light downward, increasing the intensity of light delivered to your tank.

➤ *Marine-Glo*. A bluish, near-UV bulb, great for salt-water corals and helpful for some freshwater plants. However, this bulb should be used in combination with other bulbs for best results.

➤ *Flora-Glo*. A good bulb for many types of plants. I have had some cryptocorynes really take off under this bulb. It has an orangish cast to it, though, so you may want to mix it with other bulbs to make the light more pleasing to the eye.

Got Your Tank Covered?

Now that I've talked about the bulbs, let's discuss the light fixtures. Most light fixtures also act as covers for your tank. Covering the tank is important for several reasons:

➤ It reduces evaporation. Less refilling of the tank will be required. Replacing evaporation is not a substitute for making a partial water change, though!

➤ A cover keeps the fish from jumping out onto the floor. It also helps keep crabs and frogs from climbing out.

➤ Your aquarium's top will help keep the kids and the cats out of the tank.

If, you don't feel the need for a light, or perhaps can't afford it now, you may buy a glass canopy or plastic cover alone to at least keep the fish from jumping out.

Let There Be Light

There are many ways to provide light for your aquarium. The range of light fixture styles and prices is quite wide, ranging from inexpensive full-hoods to metal-halide pendant lamps that may cost several hundred dollars. Typically, the lighting system will be the most expensive piece of equipment for your aquarium.

Full-Hoods

A full-hood is the most popular choice for covering and lighting your aquarium. It consists of a plastic chassis that has three basic sections:

1. A lid in front to access the tank

2. A glass section in the middle to protect the light strip from water damage

3. Either punch-outs or a soft plastic strip at the rear of the hood, to allow for custom openings for installing heaters, filters, and air lines

A strip light is included, and fits on top of the full-hood's chassis. There are two types of chassis. In one type (often called deluxe), there are pegs on the underside that you snap off to make the hood nest perfectly on your brand of aquarium. There are also recessed versions of hoods. Rather than resting on top of the frame, they nest down inside, on the inner lip. The one disadvantage to these is that not all aquarium frames have the same size inner lip, if any at all. So while the deluxe hoods should fit any brand of tank, the recessed hoods may not.

All sizes of full-hoods are available with fluorescent lights, with larger ones possibly having several rows of bulbs. Sizes under 30 inches, generally 29-gallon tanks and below, are also available in incandescent styles.

A full-hood light. (courtesy of All-Glass Aquarium Company)

Fluorescent full-hoods are a better choice. While they will cost a bit more than incandescent fixtures initially, fluorescent fixtures are more cost-efficient in the long run. Fluorescent lights give off a brighter, more even flood of light than incandescents. They use much less electricity, and the bulbs last longer.

Personally, I think among the choices to cover and light your aquarium, full-hoods have the nicest appearance. However, they make it difficult or impossible to add additional lights for live plants.

Strip Lights and Glass Canopies

The glass canopy functions similarly to the chassis on the full-hood. Except for the adjustable back plastic strip, the entire cover is glass, with a hinged glass panel creating a lid in front. Strip lights, which are the long plastic housings containing the light units, sit on top of the glass canopy. If you thought strip lights were mood lights for exotic dancers, then I'm sorry I got your hopes up. Most strip lights are fluorescent models, but a few small sizes of incandescent strip lights are available.

A glass canopy with a strip light. (courtesy of All-Glass Aquarium Company)

While I believe the full-hood has a neater and more decorative appearance than the glass canopy–strip light combo, I've come to prefer the latter. Why? Because it is more versatile. My favorite style of aquarium is a heavily planted one. To do it right, you need lots of light. The glass canopy allows me to easily put multiple strip lights on top to provide extra light.

Compact Fluorescents

With intense output and low energy consumption, compact flourescent units do a very good job. Typically, bulbs come in white (5,000°K and 6,500°K), and blue (7,100°K). Blue bulbs are normally used for the corals in saltwater reef tanks, but some benefit may be obtained by mixing them with white lights for planted freshwater tanks.

Compact fluorescent fixtures come two ways. One way is as an upgrade kit. That is, you get the ballast and wiring along with a polished aluminum reflector with the bulbs mounted on it. You use small screws to mount the reflector and bulbs inside the decorative wooden canopy (purchased separately) that sits on top of your tank. Fluorescent compacts also may be purchased pre-installed in decorative wooden or metal canopies that you set on top of the tank or hang above it.

Enhancing the Light

If you want to increase the output of your existing fixtures, there are ways to do so without buying new ones. Many stores carry polished aluminum reflectors that fit behind the bulb in your light unit. These take light that normally comes out the sides and top of the bulb, and direct it down toward the tank. It is not as good as adding another light, but it is an improvement.

Also, some fluorescent bulbs come with either internal or external reflective coatings on the bulb's top half. This directs more light downward. You may want to consider replacing your bulb with one of these.

Electrical Consumption

Finally, all this talk of high wattage makes this a good place to dispel a myth. The typical aquarium will have no noticeable effect on your electric bill. In most areas of the country, a 10-gallon aquarium will increase your electric bill by less than $1 per month. Larger tanks aren't much different. Your heater probably will be the item to pull the most juice at any one time, but it will almost always be off.

Chapter 6

Just a Few More Things to Buy

In This Chapter

➤ Other items you need to round out your complete setup

➤ Water conditioners and test kits

➤ A few things that you can live without but may want to pick up anyway

---

Previous chapters covered the major systems in your aquarium, including the tank, the stand, the filter system, and the heating and lighting systems—most of the items you need to properly set up your aquarium. But a few supplies remain.

Go With the Flow

If you have purchased an air pump to run an undergravel filter or to power airstones or action aerating ornaments, you will need a way to connect the air pump to those items and to regulate the flow. Various kinds of tubes are available to make the connection.

➤ *Air line.* This flexible plastic tubing, about the diameter of a soda straw, sells by the foot and cuts easily with scissors. You cut pieces of the desired length and simply snug the ends over the valves and connections to hook everything up. Most air line tubing sold in stores is clear vinyl. You also may run across green silicone rubber air tubing. In most cases, it does not make any difference which you pick.

➤ *Mini-tubing.* The diameter of this air tubing is smaller than usual. It can be used to connect action aerating ornaments. The advantage is that the smaller diameter makes the tubing less buoyant and easier to conceal. Mini-tubing comes with end connectors that adapt it to fit regular-size air tubing. You cannot connect mini-tubing directly to your air pump, valves, filter stems, or airstones. Nor would you want to. The small diameter puts more back-pressure on the diaphragm of your air pump. Use it only where you need to conceal tubing that runs to ornaments, and use regular air line tubing for all other applications.

➤ *Plant air tubing.* Perhaps even better for disguising air lines that run to ornaments is plant air tubing. Each package comes with several feet of green air line that you cut to length. Also included are several frilly sections that resemble aquatic plant leaves. You thread the leaves over the green tubing, and the result is a plastic plant with a hollow stem that allows air to pass through.

Air to Spare

Sometimes you will be able to use air lines to connect directly to the items that it will be running. However, if you need to connect to extra outlets, combine into fewer outlets, control flow, or vent excess pressure, you will need air valves to do so.

The easiest type of valve to use is a gang-valve. A gang-valve is several valves connected and mounted on a plastic or metal hanger. You can buy two-gang-, three-gang-, four-gang-, and five-gang-valves, which can run two to five outlets, respectively. You hang the assembly on the back of your tank, attach the air line from your air pump to the side input connectors of the gang-valve. Then, you connect air lines to the valves and run the output to your filters or ornaments.

Fish and Tips

Do not confuse *two-way* and *three-way* valves with *gang-valves*. A two-way valve inserts into a single line to control its output. A three-way valve adds another outlet to a gang-valve, or inserts into a single line to split off a controllable outlet.

Remember that gang-valves divide the power of your air pump—they do not multiply it. So if you use gang-valves to run more outlets, first be sure your pump is able to put out enough air to do so.

Ideally, you should put a check-valve on each outlet of your air pump (the outlets on the pump, not the outlets on the valve). The check-valve is a device that allows air to flow only one way. By placing one on each outlet, the check-valve prevents water from back-siphoning through the air lines, should a power outage occur.

Hauling in Your Catch

It helps to have a fish net. Normally, the only time you will ever want to net a fish is when it is dead. However, you never know when you may need to catch a fish to move it to another tank to breed, to recover from a fight, or to be medicated. Or maybe the fish has just outgrown the tank and you want to give it to a friend.

Sometimes the easiest way to catch fish is with two nets. Hold one in place and use the other to herd the fish into the first. You may want to buy one fine net and one coarse net. That way, you will have the right size mesh for the job and two nets when you need them.

Water Conditioners

Most aquarists need to treat their tap water to make it safe for fish. Your needs will depend on the condition of your local tap water. In Chapter 11, I'll tell you what factors to consider when shopping for a water conditioner. But right now let's look at some typical water conditioners.

Dechlorinators

If you have city water, you will have to remove the chlorine. Your aquarium store will carry several water conditioners whose main purpose is to dechlorinate tap water. Many brands also offer other benefits. For example, some will remove chloramines and heavy metals or buffer the pH a bit. Some brands even provide a "liquid bandage" factor. That is, they will produce a temporary slime coat on fish that have been damaged by being netted.

Aquarium Salt

Many hobbyists and dealers recommend that you add one teaspoon of aquarium salt per gallon of water. It helps reduce disease, and is perfectly harmless to all species of fish. If you go this route, be sure to pick up some aquarium salt at the pet store.

Fish and Tips

Even if you don't have city water, but draw water from a well, you may still want to use a water conditioner. You won't have chlorine to remove, but you may need the other features provided by the water conditioner.

Water-Softener Pillows

If hard water is a problem in your area, you may need these. Ask your dealer about local conditions. If you do use water-softener pillows, be sure to purchase a general hardness test kit. You need to be able to tell when you've softened enough.

pH Adjusters

You may not need to mess with your pH at all. It depends on your local tap water and the types of fish you want to keep. Usually, your water pH will be fine as is. It is probably the same water used by your dealer, anyway.

Tests You Don't Want to Pass

I highly recommend that you don't pass by the test kit aisle when shopping for your supplies. When problems develop, the proper test kit can often determine exactly where the problem is and what needs to be done. You can't tell the condition of your tap water by looking at it.

pH Kit

Always purchase a pH kit. There are many inexpensive and easy-to-use brands on the market. Besides measuring the pH of the water in your new tank, your pH kit can be used to monitor trends. A declining pH is usually a sign of insufficient water changes.

Ammonia and Nitrite Kits

I highly recommend these kits, as well—particularly in new tanks. In fact, the brand-new setup is the one where ammonia is most likely to be a problem. Nitrite kits are also highly recommended for new tanks.

Fishy First-Aid Kit

Usually, it is not a good idea to buy medications until you need them. Medications should not be used as preventives, and they have limited shelf lives. So if you purchase them long before you need them, they may become useless or even toxic. Besides, there's a chance you will never have to medicate your fish. So why spend the money?

However, there is one type of medication that is cheap, has a long shelf life, and wouldn't hurt to have hanging around. That medication is a malachite green or formalin-malachite green ich remedy. I will tell you a lot more about this medication in Chapter 16 on stress and disease. For now, suffice it to say that ich (pronounced *ick*) is probably the most common fish disease experienced by new hobbyists, and is quite easy to treat—if you catch it in time.

Quarantine Tank

A quarantine tank is the other item that I would recommend, although I realize that few people go to the trouble. A quarantine tank doesn't have to be fancy. A simple 5.5- or 10-gallon aquarium with a sponge filter, heater, and a couple of plastic plants for cover is all you need. You can use a quarantine tank to medicate a single sick fish, rather than treating the whole tank (sometimes). A quarantine tank is also a good place to allow an injured fish to heal. And using it to quarantine new arrivals before they ever go into your main tank can help keep disease from getting there in the first place.

You also may want to have an isolation basket on hand. There are several styles of these, usually sold as net breeders, breeding baskets, breeding traps, or isolation containers. Some are clear plastic containers with perforations to allow water to flow through. They hang inside your tank, and you put the fish that needs protection inside. The best types are the ones made of a simple plastic frame with a net mesh all around. They allow water to flow through easily.

There are coarse mesh and fine mesh models, but the coarse mesh is usually best. It allows droppings and un-eaten food to fall out of the net more easily. Of course, if you want to use the basket to protect baby fish, the fine mesh may be required.

Cleaning Supplies

There are a few items you will need for the routine maintenance of your aquarium. These items will make partial water changes and glass cleaning a snap.

Gravel Vacuum

If there is one item that will make your life easy, this is it. Gravel vacuums are quick, easy, and cheap to use. A gravel vacuum is a very simple device. It consists of a large tube attached to a siphon hose. There are no motors or moving parts. Use the gravel vacuum to siphon out water to make your partial water changes. As you do so, you poke the large tube into your gravel. The flow is strong enough to draw all the debris up out of the gravel, but not strong enough to siphon out the gravel, too. With a gravel vacuum, your partial water change gets rid of both dissolved waste and solid debris.

A gravel vacuum makes life easy for you and your fish.
(Courtesy of Tetra-Second Nature, makers of Hydro-Clean)

There is a fancier "clean-and-fill" version of this device.
Instead of having a short hose to siphon into a bucket, it
comes with a longer hose and a valve that attaches to
your sink. You can buy models with 25, 50, 75, and even
100 feet of hose. Water pressure from your sink powers
the device. When you set the valve one way, the water
pressure forms a vacuum that draws water out of your
tank. A gravel vacuum tube on the other end cleans your
gravel. When you're done, flip the valve and water flows
the other way. So, you can refill your tank right from the
faucet. Of course, you need to be sure that the new water
is the right temperature, and don't forget to add a
dechlorinator.

Algae Scrubber

Most hobbyists keep one or more algae-eating fish—and
they are very helpful—but you still may need to clean the
inside glass occasionally. Some types of algae aren't edible,
or perhaps there is just too much for the algae eaters.

Anyway, there are several styles of algae scrubbers and scrapers on the market. My favorite is a plain scrubber pad. You can buy coarse ones for glass tanks, or softer ones for acrylic tanks. You can buy algae scrubbers on a stick, but they are much harder to maneuver than the hand-held pads. There are also razor blade scrapers for the really tough types of algae. Do not use razor-blade-style algae scrapers on acrylic tanks. You may scratch the finish.

Something's Fishy

Never use soap to clean your aquarium or any items in it! Soap is extremely toxic to fish.

If you don't like to dip your hand in the water much, then (1) you are a little weird, (2) you may be in the wrong hobby, and (3) you should consider buying a magnetic algae scraper. This consists of two magnetic parts. One part, which has either embedded blades or scrubber pads, goes inside the tank. The other part goes outside the tank. The magnetic attraction keeps them together. When you move the outer piece, the inner scraper portion slides around, too. These are kind of fun, and most do a fair job, but they don't get into corners or tight spots very well.

A Bucket to Lug It

A fish bucket comes in very handy. You will need one to siphon water into when you make your partial water changes—unless you purchased one of the clean-and-fill systems. You also can use a bucket to carry replacement water back to the tank. Fish can be transported in a bucket. Plus, you can use one to hold dripping filters or filter media that you want to take to the sink for cleaning. If you ever break your tank, you may need a bucket to hold the fish while you go buy a new one. Get at least a five-gallon bucket.

Something's Fishy

Don't use your household cleaning bucket for water changes on your aquarium. Soap residue may cause problems. Instead, keep a separate bucket for aquarium use only, and make sure everyone in the house knows not to use it for other tasks.

Replacement Filter Materials

You won't need to have spares of these immediately, but it doesn't hurt to have your replacement filter media ready to go when you need it. Naturally, what you need will depend on the type of filter you buy. Be sure to ask your dealer if the initial set of filter media comes with the filter. Sometimes the media is included; sometimes you must purchase it separately. Your filter won't work without the proper media.

Buy a Book!

A good beginner's text will greatly increase your chances of success in the hobby. Naturally, I recommend that you buy *this* book. In fact, I'm pretty sure that the law requires it! Besides, when you're not busy reading it, the book is great for propping up the leg on that wobbly chair.

Chapter 7

Picking Your First Fish

In This Chapter

➤ Considering compatibility

➤ Rules to prevent overcrowding

➤ Spotting a healthy fish

➤ Brief descriptions of popular, hardy species

➤ Recommended algae-eaters and scavengers

Time to get to the exciting part! So far we have spent lots of time discussing aquariums, filters, heaters, and a bunch of other pieces of equipment, but our only interest in those gadgets is the fact that we need them to keep the fish alive. Nobody gets into the hobby because they think filters and air pumps are cool. It is all those dazzling tropical fish that are the draw. Fish! Fish! Beautiful fish!

Picking out your first batch of fish is definitely fun. But guess what? Picking them out will be one of the hardest things you will ever do. It will be hard because your dealer is going to tempt you by offering so many varieties of fish for sale that you will not be able to make up your mind. Your tank can hold only so many fish, and I'm betting that your wallet holds only so many dollars. So deciding which fish to pick is going to be tough.

Be Prepared

For starters, do your homework. Get some books and read up on various species to find information about their quirks. In this chapter, I will list many common, peaceful species that would make good starter fish in a community aquarium. With few exceptions, the fish listed here will readily mix and match with each other.

Little Fish Equals Big Snack

Remember that big fish eat little fish. Even big *peaceful* fish eat little fish. Tank mates should always be of similar size, and when deciding this, don't just look at the overall size of the fish. Consider the size of the fish's mouth, too. There are many species that can eat a tank mate that is almost the same size as themselves.

Also, be sure to allow for growth. Very few of the fish sold in the local shop are adult size. For example, did you know that a full-grown goldfish can be over a foot long? I've even heard reports of them growing to over 18 inches. Try to pick species that will grow to similar size, and at similar rates. Although clown loaches and oscars grow to about 14 inches long, if you buy them both at a one-inch size the oscar will be large enough to eat the clown loach within very few weeks.

Can't We All Just Get Along?

Unfortunately, no. We can't, and neither can fish. You can't just throw every fish that interests you into the same tank and expect them all to get along. You must pick compatible species.

Fish may fight for many reasons, but meanness is not one of them. When fish fight, they have good reason to do so. Perhaps they are protecting their home territory from squatters, or maybe they are driving off rivals who would steal their mates. They might be protecting their young from predators or reserving their favorite sleeping spot.

Your dealer can steer you toward compatible species. Often it will say right on the price tag if a species is normally aggressive. But don't be afraid to ask for advice. Also, you can usually feel free to browse in fish books that are for sale in the store. Be careful not to bend them or get them wet, though, unless you plan to buy.

Dig That Crazy Fish

Sometimes another problem comes along with territoriality. Many territorial fish like to do their own interior decorating. That is, they like to dig pits and rearrange plants. Sometimes they do it to clear a spot for breeding. Sometimes it is to make a hiding place. Some fish seem to do it just for fun. For whatever reason, you may find that your meticulously artful landscaping job gets destroyed by a fish with its own idea of what is good taste.

When picking fish, this will be another consideration. The fish don't just need to be compatible with each other. They also need to be compatible with your decorations.

Smart Fish Stay in Schools

Not all fish are territorial. Some of them like to hang out in gangs. This is not a bad thing. They aren't going to spray paint graffiti on the aquarium walls, and they won't be spending weekends at the tattoo parlor. Rather, they'll be in schools. You will find that a school of fish is a relaxing thing to watch.

Fish that are in schools are almost always on the go. Schools of fish—some call them shoals—will add action to your tank. So when you buy fish that prefer to live in schools, it is best to buy enough so that they want to behave as schooling fish. They will feel better and put on a much more interesting show for you.

How many fish make up a school? Good question. If we look at nature, schools of fish may have thousands of individuals in them. Unfortunately, we just don't have enough room to put that many fish in most tanks. So here is what I recommend. In large tanks, try to put at least a dozen fish in a school. In medium tanks, keep at least six per schooling species. In small tanks, it is going to take at least three fish to make a group. Even then, the chances are good that they won't stick together all that much. Still, keeping three of a schooling species is better than keeping onesies and twosies, because they will hide less and show less submissive color patterns.

Day Shift and Night Shift

You can have a tank full of peaceful, beautiful fish, but if they are never out when you are around, how much fun would that be? The answer is not much, unless you are *really* easily entertained. When choosing species, consider whether they are diurnal or nocturnal.

Fish School

For *diurnal* fish, lights out means time to zonk out. *Nocturnal* fish party all night and sleep all day.

I Want to Be on Top

Many species will prefer to inhabit particular strata of the tank. Most of the schooling fishes will prefer mid-water. Most scavengers will want to hang out near the bottom.

Most territorial fish will want to stake out a piece of ground, too.

However, there are exceptions. For example, the various species of gouramies are territorial, and they prefer to stay near the top of the tank. Silver hatchetfish and zebra danios like to school, but they also prefer the upper reaches of the tank. Anyway, a good mix of top, middle, and bottom dwellers will help balance the aquatic picture. There will be fewer fights, and more enjoyment for you.

Please, Sir, May I Have Some More?

Some of your fishy pets will have specialized diets, and it is up to you to see that they get their fair share. For example, a tiretrack eel will need live blackworms in its diet, if it is to prosper. Any good aquarium store will sell them. You need to be willing to provide these to keep a tiretrack eel.

Also, if you are feeding during the day but have some fish that only eat at night, can you see what may happen? When the nocturnal fish come out looking for food, there is none left. They will starve, even though you feed the fish every day. Make sure your feeding regimen allows for this. I'll talk about that more in Chapter 13.

How Many Pesos for That Pisces?

You also may want to consider the price of the fish you buy for your first batch. Believe it or not, a brand-new, sparkling clean tank is rougher on fish than an established, dirty aquarium. Check out Chapter 10 on cycling your aquarium to see why. Since your first fish are at the most risk, it is advisable to choose cheaper, hardier, species. You can add the more delicate or pricier fish a bit later.

Get Out Your Ruler

How many fish will fit in your tank? You'll get many answers to this question. Some are right. Some are wrong.

And some answers are sometimes right and sometimes wrong. Let's look at a couple of popular rules:

➤ You need 12 square inches of water surface for each one-inch length of fish.

➤ Don't keep more than one inch of fish per gallon of water.

Let's talk about that first rule. An aquarium that is 12 inches wide by 24 inches long by 16 inches high would give you 288 square inches of water surface (length times width). Take 288 and divide by 12 inches of water surface per fish, and you can see that you could keep 24 one-inch fish in that tank—or, say, 12 two-inch fish. Either way, it's a total of 24 inches of fish.

Fish and Tips

There are two ways to measure fish length. *Standard length* is the length from tip of nose to base of tail. *Total length* is measured from tip of nose to tip of tail. Use standard length to determine how many fish will fit in your tank.

Now let's look at the second rule—which, by the way, is the one that is most popular and you are most likely to be told by your dealer. It just so happens that the dimensions for the aquarium I used to discuss the first rule are the dimensions for a typical 20-gallon aquarium. According to the one-inch-per-gallon rule, a 20-gallon aquarium will hold 20 inches of fish. That is, 20 one-inch fish, or 10 two-inch fish.

It's Not So Much a Rule as a Guideline

You can see that both rules give similar results. The numbers are not that far off. However, *both rules only work for small fish up to three inches in length.* If you apply the same rules to larger fish, you will fail very quickly. One 20-inch fish would not live in either of those tanks, for example.

Here is why. Those rules only consider the length of the fish. The problem is that, when a fish grows, its height and breadth change, too. In fact, when a fish doubles its length, it is increasing its mass and volume about eight times. Technically, any change in length will cube the change in mass, or volume, of the fish. Below is a conversion chart to illustrate this for you. Notice how rapidly the change occurs.

Fish Mass

Fish Length	Equivalent in One-Inch Fish	How Many Gallons Per Fish This Size?
1 inch	1	1
2 inches	8	1
3 inches	27	1
4 inches	64	2
5 inches	125	4
6 inches	216	8*
7 inches	343	10*
8 inches	512	15*
9 inches	729	18*
10 inches	1,000	20*
11 inches	1,331	20*
12 inches	1,728	25*
24 inches	13,824	125*

These figures assume that you will make weekly partial water changes. Otherwise, waste will build up too quickly.

Notice how much difference there is between the mass of 24 one-inch fish (24) and one 24-inch fish (13,824). It is the same number of total inches in length, but the difference in fish mass units is 13,800. Yikes!

By the way, don't forget to allow for growth. A fish that is one inch long today may be four inches long in a month, or a foot long in a year.

That's Sick!

It won't do you much good to be able to pick compatible interesting fish if you can't tell a healthy one from a sick one. It only takes one sick fish to infect a whole tank and mess up your day. So let's talk about ways to spot a healthy fish. Be sure to read Chapter 16 on stress and disease for detailed descriptions of warning signs that signal a sick fish.

When you go fish shopping, look for fish with clear eyes and skin. The color should be bright and even, and there should be no unusual discoloration or bloody patches. Be sure the fish has good body weight. Avoid fish with hollow bellies and bent spines.

Watch the way they hold their fins. Healthy fish usually keep their fins fairly erect. They'll spread them even more when courting a mate or displaying to mark territory. Clamped fins (fins held folded against the body) are signs of a fish that is sick, tired, and droopy.

A healthy fish has fins with smooth edges and no splits. Ragged edges may be a sign of disease, or a sign that the fish has been bullied. Split fins are generally the results of fights, too. A split fin or two is not usually a big deal. Split fins heal quickly. But a ragged-looking fish has been through too much already.

Look for fish that exhibit behavior and coloration that is normal for the species. For example, if a species likes to

school, avoid the fish hanging around in the corner away
from the rest of the group.

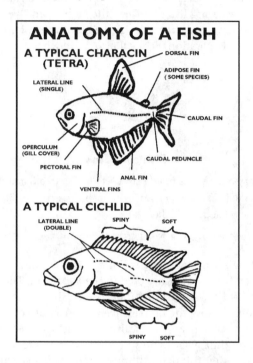

Note the activity level of the fish. Does it show an interest
in life? Avoid lethargic specimens of normally active species, but be aware that it is normal behavior for many fish
to sit there and do nothing most of the time.

Avoid purchasing from tanks that contain fish showing
signs of stress or illness. Particularly avoid tanks that contain dead fish. Note the color of the water in the tank.
Discolored water probably means the fish are sick and the
tank is under medication.

Okay, that's enough about how to pick fish. Let's move on
to which fish to pick.

Algae-Eaters

Every tank probably should have some sort of algae-eating fish. Algae-eating fish help keep the glass clean—yes, they do windows—and they help keep algae off the plants, rocks, and decorations. They'll also scavenge for uneaten foods.

Fish and Tips

It may not be wise to add algae-eating fish to a brand new aquarium. There won't yet be enough algae to keep them fed and happy. Add them later.

The algae-eating species that I'm about to list are egglayers, not commonly bred in the aquarium. They are all peaceful toward fish of other species, though they may fight a bit among themselves. They need a fair amount of vegetation to stay at peak health, so consider offering some Spirulina algae tablets in addition to the foods you offer the other fish. Plecostomus will munch away at the driftwood in your tank, too.

➤ Chinese Algae-Eater (*Gyrinocheilus aymonieri*)

➤ Otocinclus (*Otocinclus* spp.), pronounced *oh-toh-SINK-lus*

➤ Plecostomus (*Hypostomus plecostomus*, *Ancistrus* spp., *Xenocara* spp., and others), pronounced *pleh-COST-oh-mus*

➤ Whiptail Cat (*Loricaria* spp.)

➤ Stick Cat (*Farlowella* spp.), also called twig cat

➤ Siamese Flying Fox (*Epalzeorhynchus siamensis*). This fish is also called the Siamese algae-eater, but that name is sometimes confused for the Chinese algae-eater. Also, don't confuse it with the regular flying fox, *Epalzeorhynchus kalopterus*.

➤ Borneo Sucker (*Pseudogastromyzon myersi*). This fish is also sold as the Hong Kong pleco, Myer's hillstream loach, and butterfly pleco.

Barbs

This fish has small whiskers, called barbels (*BAR-buls*), at the corners of its mouth, which is where it gets its name. Barbs are generally peaceful, and most of the varieties that are available stay small enough to keep in a typical community tank. Barbs are egglayers, are active during the day, and prefer to live in schools. The males are usually more colorful, and the females are usually heavier bodied. Barbs are great choices if you are looking for mid-water swimmers.

➤ Tiger Barb (*Capoeta tetrazona*)

➤ Gold Barb (*Puntius sachsi*)

➤ Checkerboard Barb (*Capoeta oligolepsis*)

➤ Cherry Barb (*Capoeta titteya*)

➤ Black Ruby Barb (*Puntius nigrofasciatus*)

➤ Rosy Barb (*Puntius conchonius*)

➤ Tinfoil Barb (*Barbodes schwanenfeldii*)

Catfish

There are many species of catfish available for the aquarium. Some are peaceful scavengers. Some are vicious predators. You want the former, unless you are planning to mix it with other fish of similar size and aggression.

Another benefit of the peaceful scavenger varieties of catfish is that they are more likely to be active during the day. So they are more fun to watch.

➤ Corydoras Cat (*Corydoras* spp.), pronounced *kor-ee-DOR-us*. The bronze cat (*C. aeneus*), leopard cat (*C. julii*), and skunk cat (*C. arcuatus*) are some popular subspecies. There are also some albino cory cats available.

➤ Armored Cat (*Callichthys* spp., *Hoplosternum* spp., *Dianema* spp.)

➤ Raphael Cat, which includes the striped raphael cat (*Platydoras costatus*), the spotted raphael cat (*Agamyxis pectinifrons*), and the talking cat (*Amblydoras hancocki*).

➤ Upside-Down Cat (*Synodontis nigriventris*)

➤ Glass Catfish (*Kryptopterus bicirrhis*)

➤ Polka Dot Cat (*Pimelodus pictus*)

Fish and Tips

Usually, catfish with small mouths and short whiskers will be peaceful scavengers, active during the day. Those with large mouths and long flowing whiskers are usually predatory, and are more likely to be nocturnal.

Cichlids

Pronounced *SICK-lids,* this group of fish includes a large array of species. Almost all are territorial and therefore aggressive to at least some degree. Most fish that get big and mean are members of this group, but there are species that are suitable for the typical community tank.

➤ Angelfish (*Pterophyllum scalare*)

➤ Kribensis (*Pelvicachromis pulcher*), pronounced *krih-BEN-sis*

➤ Ram (*Microgeophagus ramirezi*)

Danios

Pronounced *DAN-ee-os*, this group of fish is one of the most popular. They are bred in huge quantities on commercial farms, so the price is very low. Danios are also among the hardiest of fishes and, being highly active, they will add action to any tank. To best enjoy them, keep them in schools.

➤ Zebra Danio (*Brachydanio rerio*)

➤ Pearl Danio (*Brachydanio albolineatus*)

➤ Leopard Danio (*Brachydanio frankei*)

➤ Giant Danio (*Danio malabaricus*)

➤ White Cloud Mountain Minnow (*Tanichthys albonubes*)

Eels

Some fish labeled as eels are not eels at all. In fact, some are not even fish. Additionally, most true eels are very poor choices for the aquarium because they are highly predatory, prefer saltwater, and present other problems. However, there are some eels suitable for freshwater aquariums.

➤ Spiny Eels (*Mastacembelus* spp. and *Macrognathus* spp.)

Goldfish

This fish has been bred for ponds, bowls, and aquaria for hundreds of years. It is the first fish that was ever kept for decorative purposes. Personally, I don't recommend keeping goldfish with the other tropical fish listed in this book. Goldfish prefer cooler water, a slightly different diet, and tend to outgrow most of the species listed here. Also, most varieties are slow moving and long-finned, which makes them easy targets for other faster, slightly nippy fish.

There are too many varieties of goldfish to list them all. Though the varieties may look quite different, they are all of the same species, *Carassius auratus*. You will find that price varies according to size, variety, and origin. The cheapest fish will be raised in the United States. The fish from China will have better color and body shape (and cost more), and Japanese stock will be even better and more expensive.

➤ Common Goldfish and Comet Goldfish

➤ Shubunkin

➤ American Fantail

➤ Calico Fantail

➤ Black Moor

➤ Celestial Eye

➤ Bubble Eye

➤ Oranda

➤ Lionhead or Ranchu

Gouramies

Pronounced *go-RAH-mees*. There are quite a few unique things about this group of fish. For starters, they have a special chamber in their gills, called the labyrinth. It allows these fish to grab a bubble of air from the surface and breathe from it, thereby surviving in places where other fish would suffocate due to low levels of dissolved oxygen in the water. Because of the labyrinth, gouramies can often survive quite well in fish bowls.

These fish usually live in shallow, weedy water, such as ditches. Since they live where there are many weeds but not much water, they tend to be protective of their space. All gouramies are territorial to some extent, and particularly toward their own species. Another interesting thing about this group of fish is that most build bubble nests when they spawn. The feeler-like pectoral fins are another interesting feature.

➤ Dwarf Gourami (*Colisa lalia*)

➤ Honey Dwarf Gourami (*Colisa sota*, formerly *C. chuna*)

➤ Giant Gourami (*Colisa fasciata*)

➤ Kissing Gourami (*Helostoma temmincki*)

➤ Pearl Gourami (*Trichogaster leeri*)

➤ Blue Gourami (*Trichogaster trichopterus*)

Guppies

The good old guppy was one of the very first fish kept in aquariums. It stays small, it is very hardy, and the males are sprinkled with many colors. Additionally, no two seem to be exactly alike. Even better, this fish is a livebearer, so it is very easy to breed. The anal fin of mature males changes into a tube, called the gonopodium, that is able to internally fertilize the females. Males will spend much of their day courting the ladies. It is best to keep at least two females for each male, so that the females will get some occasional rest.

➤ Common Guppy (*Poecilia reticulata*)

➤ Fancy Guppy (*Poecilia reticulata*)

Hatchetfish

The marble hatchet (*Carnegiella strigata*), the black-lined silver hatchet (*Gasteropelecus sternicla*), and the silver hatchet (*Thoracocharax securis*) are all commonly available. These fish, with their unusual shape, are definitely surface dwellers. They're a great choice for filling in the top zone of an aquarium. Keep the tank covered, because they're excellent jumpers.

Loaches

The various species of loaches come in different body shapes. Some look like worms and some are more torpedo shaped. What they have in common is a spine beneath each eye, which can be erected to use as a weapon. It's a good idea to be careful handling this fish when you net it, particularly larger specimens, or you could get jabbed. Many fishes in this family are called botias, pronounced *boh-TEE-yas*. The ones labeled as loaches are usually peaceful, while the species with the word botia in the common name have a tendency to get nippy with other fish.

➤ Coolie Loach (*Acanthophthalmus kuhlii, A. semicinctus*)

➤ Dojo Loach (*Misgurnus anguillicaudatus*)

➤ Clown Loach (*Botia macracantha*)

➤ Yo-Yo Loach (*Botia lohachata*)

➤ Horseface Loach (*Acanthopsis choirorhynchus*)

Fish and Tips

Clown loaches will commonly lie down when resting. People often see the fish on its side and mistakenly think it is sick.

Mollies

This livebearing fish (*Poecilia latipinna, P. sphenops, P. velifera*) is available in several varieties. There are silver, black, gold, and marble colorations. One black-spotted silver version has appropriately earned the name dalmatian molly. The males of some species have a large sailfin that they splay during courtship or territorial display. In the wild, mollies are found in coastal areas. As with all livebearers, you should keep at least two females for each male. Schenops mollies grow to around two inches; the others grow to six inches.

Fish and Tips

Mollies do best if you add one to two teaspoons of aquarium salt per gallon of water. In fact, mollies can even tolerate pure seawater. They also prefer temperatures around 80°F (27°C) and extra vegetation in the diet.

Paradise Fish

(*Macropodus opercularis*) This fish is red and blue striped, with a red tail. It is attractive, but more aggressive than most in the gourami family, so I don't recommend it for small tanks. However, it is an excellent choice to keep alone in a fish bowl, much the way male bettas are often kept. Paradise fish will fare much better in a bowl than a goldfish, because goldfish don't have the labyrinth in their gills.

Piranhas

(*Serrasalmus* spp.) What can I say? Piranhas are tetras, too. However, you should *never* mix them with other fish. Keep piranhas *only* in dedicated piranha tanks. Piranhas are eating machines. The truth is that they are not very aggressive—in fact, you will usually find them to be quite shy in the aquarium. Many species are plenty tough enough to beat them up. However, piranhas have teeth that can bite through flesh as easily as any razor blade. So they can easily dismantle fish that are larger than themselves.

Platies

Pronounced *PLAT-ees* (*Xiphophorus maculatus*), they are sometimes also called moons. The blue moon is the closest thing to the wild coloration of this fish. Humans have selectively bred many other varieties, though, including gold ones and bright red ones. The red wag platy, with its solid red body and black fins, is one of my favorites. Platies are livebearers, growing to a bit over two inches in length.

Rainbowfish

Rainbows are a group of fish from Australia and New Guinea. They are hardy and active, and most prefer a little aquarium salt in the water.

➤ Australian Rainbow (*Melanotaenia splendida*)

➤ Banded Rainbow (*Melanotaenia trifasciata*)

➤ Blue and Yellow Rainbow (*Melanotaenia boesemani*)

➤ Turquoise Rainbow (*Melanotaenia lacustris*)

➤ Red Irian Rainbow (*Glossolepis incisus*)

➤ Threadfin Rainbow (*Iriatherina werneri*)

Rasboras

Pronounced *Raz-BOR-uhs*, this group consists of several quite different body shapes. All like to school and tend to stay in the middle or top zones of the tank.

➤ Harlequin Rasbora (*Rasbora heteromorpha*)

➤ Brilliant Rasbora (*Rasbora borapetensis*)

➤ Scissortail Rasbora (*Rasbora trilineata*)

Sharks

There are many species that fall into this group. None of them are true sharks. True sharks live only in saltwater. These fish have gotten the name "shark" for a couple of reasons. First, the shape of the dorsal fin is like that of a shark, but mostly I suspect that the name just helps them sell better. It would be more accurate to call most of them carp, but that is not so enticing.

➤ Red-Tail Shark (*Labeo bicolor*)

➤ Rainbow Shark (*Labeo erythrurus*)

➤ Tricolor Shark (*Balantiocheilos melanopterus*)

➤ Iridescent Shark (*Pangasius sutchi*)

Something's Fishy

The black shark (*Morulius chrysophekadion*) is very similar to the red-tail and rainbow sharks, though without any red fins. Avoid this fish. They grow to 18 inches in length and are quite a bit more aggressive.

Siamese Fighting Fish

(*Betta splendens*) Also known as the betta—pronounced *BET-uh*—this fish is often well-known even to non-hobbyists. The males fight with each other, the females fight with each other, and a male may kill a female that is unwilling to mate. So it is best not to keep more than one of this species in any tank. They will mix with most other fish, though. The popular belief that they will fight to the death is incorrect. However, the resulting injuries often lead to infections that lead to death.

Fish and Tips

If you really want to see male bettas in full display, put a mirror up to the glass. When they see their own reflections, they put on quite a show for their "rival."

Males are more popular because they develop long, flowing fins and come in several bright colors. Be careful what you mix them with, though, because this is a slow-moving fish and the long fins are easy targets for any species that likes to nip. Also, bettas will sometimes attack other species that have similar colors.

Silver Dollars

(*Metynnis* spp.) Several species sell under this name. They all are silver and coin-shaped. Some species grow to eight inches, so they are not the best choice for all aquariums. Also, they like to eat live plants. It is good to provide some algae flakes in addition to the usual diet, if you keep these fish.

Swordtails

There are several strains of these *Xiphophorus helleri* available, including red velvet, red wag, gold, black, pineapple, green, and marigold swordtails. The male has a large, pointed extension on his tail that gives the fish its name. They're quite similar to platies, but with more elongated bodies. These are livebearers, so keep at least two females for each male.

Tetras

Pronounced *TEH-truhs*. Some of the most popular fish fall into this group, also known as the characins (*KARE-uh-sins*). If you want to see the best color and most peaceful behavior from these fish, be sure to keep them in schools.

➤ Neon Tetra (*Paracheirodon innesi*)

➤ Cardinal Tetra (*Paracheirdon axelrodi*)

➤ Black Tetra (*Gymnocorymbus ternetzi*)

➤ Serpae Tetra (*Hyphessobrycon serpae*)

➤ Glowlight Tetra (*Hemigrammis erythrozonus*)

➤ Head-n-Tail Light (*Hemigrammis ocellifer*)

➤ Black Neon Tetra (*Hyphessobrycon herbertaxelrodi*)

➤ Bloodfin Tetra (*Aphyocharaz anisitsi*)

➤ Red-Eye Tetra (*Moenkhausia sanctaefilomenae*)

Variatus

These livebearers (*Xiphophorus variatus*) are very similar to platies and swordtails, with a body shape about halfway between the two.

Chapter 8

Popular Plant Picks

In This Chapter

➤ Hardy plants for beginners

➤ Species with special requirements

➤ Plants to avoid

Shopping for live aquarium plants can be almost as much fun as shopping for fish. There are over 100 species of plants available, in all shapes and colors. You can find plants with feathery leaves, ribbon-shaped leaves, heart-shaped leaves, leaves like pine needles, and more. Colors range from chartreuse and emerald green to brick red and brilliant scarlet. You can mix and match to build a spectacular landscape.

Don't Get Soaked

Unfortunately, many plants that dealers carry are terrestrial, not aquatic. Don't be surprised to find common houseplants being mistakenly sold as aquatics. It is not uncommon to find bella palms and peace lilies (sold as Brazilian swords) drowning in aquariums at pet shops. Your dealer may not know better, so it will be up to you to do a little research before purchasing plants. Don't get soaked by buying non-aquatic plants!

Generally speaking, any plant that flops over lazily when removed from the water is probably a true aquatic. Any plant that can support its own weight out of the water is probably a terrestrial species, though it may be a species that thrives in both submersed and emersed conditions. Swordplants and cryptocorynes are two examples.

I will point you toward some plant species that are almost completely idiot proof. These are species that most people can successfully keep and grow. They tend to be more tolerant of water conditions, and more able to sustain themselves with lower light levels. However, don't let that be an incentive for you to reduce the amount of lights you buy. Even these hardy species will fare much better under stronger light.

Hardy Plants by the Bunch

Many of the hardiest and most readily available varieties are types of *bunch* plants. Most of these species are very fast growers, making them quite inexpensive. Most are grown on aquatic plant farms, but there are some species that are commercially harvested from wild stock in rivers in Florida and other locations.

Bunch plants may be true aquatics or species that can grow both in and out of the water. Usually dealers offer the aquatic form, but sometimes it is the terrestrial form that is sold. The tough terrestrial leaves probably will be shed after the plant is underwater for a time. By the time that happens, you will be ready to prune the old growth from the bottom and replant the top with its newer, softer submersed-form leaves.

Fish School

Bunch plant refers to seven or eight stems of a plant (clippings, actually) bound with a rubber band or strip of tape to form a bundle. The stems can be planted individually or in a group.

Following are some of my favorite varieties of bunch plants:

➤ *Anacharis Anacharis* (pronounced *uh-NAK-uh-riss*)

➤ Hornwort (*Ceratophyllum demersum* and *Ceratophyllum submersum*)

➤ *Hygro Hygrophila* (pronounced *hy-GROF-il-uh*) *polysperma*

➤ Water Wisteria *(Hygrophila difformis)*

➤ *Rotala Indica* or *Rotala rotundifolia*

➤ Java Moss *(Vesicularia dubyana)*

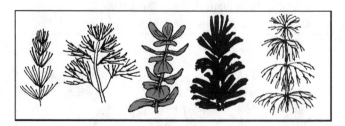

Bunch plants are fast growing and inexpensive. The stems can be planted individually or in groups.

Delicate Choices

Following are some common aquatic plants that can do well in planted aquariums, if you meet their special requirements. Providing the proper amount of light and fertilization is even more important with these species.

➤ Cabomba spp.

➤ Ambulia (*Limnophila* spp.)

➤ Foxtail (*Myriophyllum* spp.)

➤ Ludwigia (*Ludwigia repens* and *L. palustrus*)

Majestic Crown Plants

Crown plants are species with all the leaves radiating from a central base, like the points on a crown. Usually dealers sell the plants individually, but you also can find potted versions that may have several plants in one pot.

➤ Amazon Swordplant *(Echinodorus bleheri)*

➤ Pygmy Chain Sword *(Echinodorus tenellus)*

➤ Ruby Swordplant *(Echinodorus osirus var. rubra)*

➤ Vallisneria spp.

➤ Sagittaria spp.

➤ Onion Bulb Plant *(Crinum thaianum)*

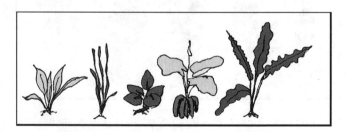

Some common crown plants, left to right: amazon sword, vallisneria, anubias nana, banana plant, and cryptocorynes.

➤ Anubias spp.

➤ Java Fern *(Microsorium pterops)*

➤ Aponogeton spp.

➤ Underwater Banana Plant *(Nymphoides aquatica)*

➤ Cryptocoryne spp.

Floating Above It All

Many species of plants have evolved to live at the water's surface. They spread their leaves across the top, with small roots dangling into the water. I find floating plants to be very beautiful, but they may not be the best choice for most aquariums. You see, floating at the surface, they block the light needed by the other plants. Also, they tend to be a very fast-spreading species. So if you keep them, be sure to thin them out regularly.

➤ Water Sprite *(Ceratopteris pteroides)*

➤ Duckweed

Weed These Out

Naturally, it would not be too smart to pick plants that are sick. Here are warning signs:

➤ Avoid plants with rotting stems. It is okay if the rot is only where the rubber band is holding bunch plants together. You can cut that part off.

➤ Shy away from specimens that are shedding leaves excessively. However, normal handling is going to break a few loose. That is not a problem.

➤ If the leaves have yellow spots, those leaves are dying. It may be due to damage, disease, or lack of fertilizer. A swordplant with six good leaves and one bad one isn't an issue, though. Simply remove the single bad leaf.

Giant Hygro

Giant hygro (*Hygrophila corymbosa*, sometimes listed as *Nomaphila stricta*) is very similar in appearance to *H. polysperma*, except that it has much larger leaves (three inches long) and a woodier stem. Giant hygro requires very strong light. While some books give this plant high marks, they always seem to show pictures of it with tough terrestrial leaves!

Other No-Nos

Many additional terrestrial houseplants are sold as aquarium plants. Those plants absolutely will not survive for long underwater. Do not buy the following species!

➤ Dracaena

➤ Dragon's Flame

➤ Red, Green, or Variegated Sanderiana

➤ Red Crinkle

➤ Purple Waffle

➤ "Bella" Palms

➤ Florida Beauty

➤ Aluminum Plant

➤ Mondo Grass

➤ Dwarf Mondo Grass

➤ Acorus Grass

➤ Gold Dust Croton

➤ Nephthytis *(Syngonium)* "Arrowhead"

➤ Brazilian Sword (Peace Lily) *(Spathiphyllum)*

➤ Princess Pine (It's hedge clippings, folks!)

Chapter 9

Welcoming Home Your Fish and Plants

In This Chapter

➤ How to acclimate your fish to their new home

➤ Tips on planting your aquarium plants

➤ How to transport your fish, if you ever move

When you buy fish from your dealer, you obviously need a way to get them home. Your dealer will provide everything you need. The dealer will place your selected fish in plastic bags that he will either seal with a rubber band or by tying the top in a knot. The bag should be fully inflated, so that it holds its shape and is less easily squashed. If the bag is flaccid, it is easier for fish to get trapped in the corners and squashed.

It's best to make fish shopping your last stop, and go straight home after you buy them. Transporting your fish home is fairly straightforward. The main precaution you must take is to be sure the fish and plants are protected from temperature extremes. If you are comfortable, then the fish are probably comfortable, too.

In hot weather, be very careful about setting the fish anyplace where they might cook. Do not set your fish on the dashboard or leave them in the trunk. Try not to set them on a seat that is getting direct sunlight. Placing the fish on the floor in the shade is a better choice. Also, don't put the fish too near an air-conditioning duct or they will get chilled.

In cold weather, be careful not to set the fish too close to the heating ducts, or they may cook quite readily.

Acclimating New Arrivals

Ideally, all new specimens should be quarantined for two weeks before they are introduced into your tank. This helps prevent the introduction of diseases. If you want to learn how to set up a quarantine tank, see Chapter 16 on disease and stress. For now, though, we will assume that this is your very first batch of fish. So your main tank can act as a quarantine tank this one time.

You probably will be quite anxious to get your new fish into the tank, but you cannot just dump them right in. The temperature and water quality in the bag may be quite different from that in your aquarium. So you must acclimate the fish. Whether you choose to use a quarantine tank, or to put fish directly into your community tank, there are several popular methods for acclimating fish to their new home.

All begin by floating the plastic fish bag on top of the water in your tank for 20 minutes. This will allow the temperatures to equalize. There is no need to float longer than this, because the temperature should be equalized by then, and there is a limited amount of oxygen in the fish bag.

The Float and Dump Method

This method is probably the most popular. It involves floating the unopened fish bag as described above, and then dumping the contents into the aquarium. It's quick. It's easy. But there is a bit more risk of shock to your fish and transmission of disease. Your fish will be going from one type of water to another with no adjustment, and if the dealer's water is carrying parasites, you have just introduced them into your tank.

The Float and Net Method

Float and net is a little better. Again, float the unopened fish bag, but instead of dumping the bag into the tank, gently net each fish out of the bag and place it in the tank. It will still be an instantaneous change from one type of water to another, but there will be a bit less chance of introducing disease to your tank. Discard the dealer's water.

The Float and Mix Method

Even better is the float and mix method. While the fish bag is floating, you open it up and pour a bit of water from your tank into the bag every few minutes. This will provide a more gradual change in water quality for your fish. After 20 minutes, you can either dump the contents into the tank, or better, gently net the fish from the bag, place the fish in the tank, and discard the water in the bag.

The Float and Drip Method

The best method of all, the drip method is merely a more methodical version of the float and mix method. The difference is, instead of adding water to the fish bag in stages, you place the fish and the water from the bag into a container on the floor. Then, using a piece of air line with a valve on it, you siphon water from your tank at a slow drip into the container on the floor. This makes the smoothest transition in water quality for the fish. When the container is full, or after 20 minutes (whichever comes first), net each fish and place it in the aquarium. Throw away the water in the container. *If you use the drip method, don't walk away and forget it, or you'll have a flood on your hands . . . er . . . floor.*

Something's Fishy

Do not feed new arrivals until they have been in the tank for a few hours or more. New fish are under stress and are unlikely to eat, so most of the food will be wasted. You will just end up polluting the tank. Be patient!

Testing the Water

One thing you also may want to do is to run a full complement of tests on your dealer's water. You can take a sample from the fish bag (before mixing your tank water into it, of course), and check the pH, ammonia, and nitrite levels. It is always interesting to see what kind of water the new fish are coming from.

Ammonia and nitrite levels should be zero, but the pH is the one that concerns us most. If it is radically different from the pH of your tank, you may want to use some sodium bicarbonate or sodium biphosphate to adjust the pH of your aquarium before adding the new fish—to prevent shock. Again, I am talking about the very first batch of fish going into the tank. If you are adding fish to an existing tank, it would not be wise to change the pH of, say, 20 fish that are already in the tank so as to make it more comfortable for one new one. It would be better to stress one than 20!

If your tank's pH is well above 7.0, particularly if it is above 7.5, you may want to add a bit of sodium biphosphate to bring the pH level closer to neutral (7.0), anyway. I'll talk a lot more about water quality, water testing, pH, and other parameters in Chapter 11.

Monitoring New Inhabitants

Once you release the new fish into the tank, you probably will want to sit and watch them for a while. Don't expect them to display much interesting behavior at first, though. New fish will be scared and tired. Many of them will want to rest and hide. Others, being in unfamiliar territory, go into a restless exploratory mode. No matter, the key thing is to observe everyone and keep your eye out for problems. Hopefully, you have picked compatible species.

Any problems that you encounter probably will not occur right away. There probably will be no aggression until everyone settles. Keep your eye out for serious fights. An occasional joust to jockey for territory or assert one's rights is not a big deal. If damage starts getting done, then corrective action may be necessary.

Fish and Tips

When introducing fish to an existing tank, it may help to feed the existing fish before introducing the new fish. Hungry fish are more likely to be aggressive.

The New Guy in Town

If you are adding fish to an existing tank, it may be a bit tougher for the fish. The established fish will have their territories already staked out. The new arrival must fight its way into a territory. So keep an especially close eye when adding to an existing tank.

Don't let me scare you too much, though. There is no need to remove a fish at the first bite. You have to give them time to work out their differences. Just don't let it progress to the point where someone gets seriously wounded or killed.

One thing you can do to help is to rearrange decorations in the tank when adding new fish. Moving the rocks and driftwood around, for example, will force existing inhabitants to find new territories, too. That way, the new guy won't be at such a disadvantage.

Keep an extra watch out for disease the first week. Fish are under the most stress when introduced to a new tank, and new fish may bring disease with them. Take time to notice changes and follow the advice in Chapter 16 (on disease and stress) if you need to.

Something's Fishy

The most important rule in moving aquariums is *never* move an aquarium that is full. Most tanks are too heavy for that, anyway, but even smaller tanks will twist and break more easily when full.

Have Bucket, Will Travel

A time may come when you need to move your aquarium, or transport your fish. Perhaps you are moving to a new house and the whole setup needs to be relocated, or maybe you just have a fish that has grown too large and your dealer is willing to take it in trade. With a little planning, the chore shouldn't be too difficult.

Moving Your Tank

Moving your aquarium to a new location may be quite easy or more difficult. A few factors come into play:

➤ Size of the tank

➤ Distance of the move

➤ Stairs!

For short moves, be they across town or just across the room, smaller tanks are much easier to manage. The easiest way to move small tanks is to drain them down to where the water just covers the fish, and then pick the whole thing up and transfer it. Refill the tank at the destination. Plants and fish remain in place, though you may temporarily need to remove rocks or driftwood that might fall and crush the fish.

This method can work with bigger tanks, too, but the chances of your being able to safely lift the weight is in question. Some large aquariums may take six people to carry them *when empty!* Also, bigger tanks often have bigger fish, which means more water is required to keep the fish covered. That is not good. You need the water to be very shallow if you plan to move the tank with fish and decor intact.

When moving a tank, don't forget to consider staircases that may be along the way—especially if you try moving the tank with decorations or fish intact. Will you be able to carry the tank up the stairs without tilting it? Tilting a tank with water in it is a very good way to break the seams of a tank, because you shift all the stress to one end or corner. Worse, if you are already struggling to handle the weight, what do you think will happen when you tilt the tank and the water sloshes to one end, putting all the weight there? Disaster!

If you move an aquarium that is too large for one person to carry easily, it is probably best to empty it completely, and carry it that way. If necessary, use a hand-truck or appliance cart to move the tank up the stairs. (Stand the empty tank on its end on the hand-truck.) You can rent hand-trucks and appliance carts at any place that rents trucks and vans.

Chapter 10

Cycling Your New Aquarium

Please read this chapter very carefully. It could make the difference between getting your tank off to a good start or getting it off on the wrong foot. The environment that you set up in an aquarium is always a fragile thing, but it is especially fragile in a new tank. This is because a balance needs to be achieved between the waste your fish excrete and the helpful bacteria that live in the tank. Earlier in the book, I mentioned that you cannot add a full load of fish all at once. You are about to learn why that is and how cycling or breaking in a new tank can prevent problems.

Good-Guy Bacteria

The first thing you need to understand is that every healthy, established aquarium is heavily populated by helpful bacteria. These good-guy bacteria are essential to the proper functioning of your aquarium. They break down ammonia and other fish waste. Without them, fish waste quickly builds up to levels that are lethal to your fish. Eventually, all the solid surfaces in your aquarium—including the gravel, glass, rocks, plant leaves, and debris—will be coated with jillions of helpful bacteria.

The problem is that when you first set up your tank these helpful bacteria are not present in sufficient quantity. The bacteria won't develop until after you have added your first batch of fish. That is because the fish produce the ammonia that is the food for the bacteria. Without ammonia to feed them, the bacteria don't multiply.

That is why a new tank is a more fragile environment than an older, established aquarium. Until you add fish, the bacteria won't develop, but until the bacteria develop, the fish continue to excrete ammonia that won't all be broken down. So the time between the initial introduction of fish and the development of full colonies of helpful bacteria is a very dangerous one.

It may seem weird, but a fish is much more likely to die of high waste levels in a brand-new, sparkling clean tank, than in an older, established, somewhat dirty tank. That's because there are enough helpful bacteria in the established tank. Now, don't take this to mean that you shouldn't keep a clean tank! On the contrary, performing the routine maintenance that keeps your tank clean is very important. Clean tanks are good, but sterile tanks are bad.

Over a period of weeks, your tank will develop plenty of helpful bacteria. The time lag between the introduction of fish and the final catch-up of waste-neutralizing bacteria is called the break-in period. We also say that we are cycling a new tank, as we progress through this period. The term derives from the nitrogen cycle, which is what is happening chemically during this process.

It Depends on the Bioload

How long does it take to cycle a new tank? Well, every aquarium is different. There are many factors that influence how long it will take to break in a new tank, but it will probably come down to two things:

1. How big is the initial bioload of the tank?

2. Did you do anything to seed the filter bed with helpful bacteria?

The bioload of your tank refers to the waste-producing plants and animals, and is obviously going to be determined most by how many living things you put in there. Wastes from these plants and animals must be removed or neutralized to keep a system healthy. Plants probably won't add much to the bioload because they don't typically produce waste products that we worry about. The exception to that is dead, decaying leaves. The fish, and any other critters, will be the main bioload in the tank. Obviously, if you put more fish into the tank, more waste will be produced, and that will result in a higher bioload.

While you may use the number of fish to judge how large a bioload your system has, when it comes right down to it, the fish really aren't the problem. *You* are the problem. And who puts the food into the tank? That's right, *you* do. Always remember that you are not just feeding the fish—you are feeding the tank.

Speeding the Process

The easiest, cheapest, and most effective way to speed the cycling process is to seed your aquarium with some gravel from an established tank. Established tanks are fully colonized by helpful bacteria. Mix the cycled gravel in with your new gravel, and your aquarium will quickly develop all the good-guy bacteria that it needs.

Where do you get some seeded gravel to add to your tank? If you have another aquarium, you can take some from there; or maybe a friend will give you some from their tank. Some dealers will give you a free handful or two, and some will sell you some out of their tanks. I wish all dealers would make cycled gravel available to their customers. Ask your dealer to see if he offers it.

Fish and Tips

If your dealer doesn't normally sell used gravel out of his tanks, offer to buy a new bag of gravel and trade it for some used gravel. This is good for both of you, because you get some gravel with bacteria to seed your tank, and he gets to freshen up the appearance of his tanks by trading some possibly worn looking gravel for some newer stuff.

Another way to speed the process is to add lots of live plants to your tank. They will be coated with well-established colonies of helpful bacteria. You can also speed up your tank's cycle by using filter media from an existing aquarium. Filter media will be coated with lots of helpful bacteria. So swapping some media from an established filter into your new filter can be a big help.

There are some products on the market that claim to contain helpful bacteria in a dormant state. Adding these products to your tank is supposed to speed up the cycle.

I must say, however, that I don't have much faith in these products. When I've tried them, I've seen little difference. Some contain enzymes that, while they will break down ammonia, don't actually seed your tank with the helpful bacteria you need. Others contain the wrong kind of bacteria. Additionally, there is the question of shelf life. My recommendation is to save your money and skip these products.

Safe Cycling

The most important quality needed for cycling a new tank is patience. You cannot rush this procedure, or you risk killing all your fish.

Okay, let's assume you have your new tank set up and running. You've given it 24 hours to make sure the temperature is stable, the tank doesn't leak, and all the equipment is functioning normally. You are ready to add your first batch of fish. To play it safe, you must assume there are no helpful bacteria in your tank, even if you've added plants or gravel from an existing tank.

Until you know the tank has sufficient good-guy bacteria, what steps do you take to ensure that ammonia won't build to toxic levels? The most important thing is not to get too excited and put too many fish in at once. An established aquarium can typically hold one inch of fish per gallon of water. When cycling a new tank, though, don't exceed *one-half inch* per gallon. If you start with fewer fish, and feed only lightly, less ammonia will be produced. This will provide ammonia to grow the helpful bacteria without letting ammonia levels get so high that they poison the fish. Later, you will be able to add more fish to your community tank.

You are probably wondering how long this process will take. As I mentioned before, each tank is different. To know for sure, you must monitor the rise and fall of ammonia and nitrite levels with water test kits. I'll discuss them in more detail in a bit. For now, a general rule is: It will take two to three weeks to cycle most tanks. However, I have seen some tanks take over a month to cycle.

There is one method of cycling an aquarium that is totally safe, but it requires even more patience. Instead of letting your fish add the ammonia that the helpful bacteria need to develop in the tank, you can add the ammonia directly. Most aquarium stores will sell some products that contain ammonium chloride for seeding new tanks. You also can use ammonia from the grocery store, though you need to get the plain stuff, not lemon scented or whatever. However, I couldn't tell you how much of the household stuff to add. It's better to get the ammonium chloride from the pet store and carefully follow the instructions on the package.

The way this process works is that you add the ammonium chloride and monitor your ammonia and nitrite levels. By monitoring those levels, you will be able to tell when the tank has cycled. At that point, you do a major water change and then add your fish. You can add them all at once because your tank will be cycled.

Now, remember that I said this method requires patience? That is because you cannot add a single fish until *after* the entire process is complete, or you risk killing the fish. Let me say that again: This method involves cycling the tank—probably for around three weeks—*without* the fish.

Finally, it is not uncommon to lose fish while cycling a new tank. If it happens to you, don't feel too badly because it happens to many people. However, if you follow the guidelines that I've presented, you have a very good chance of having every fish survive the process. If things go wrong, don't be afraid to seek help.

The Nitrogen Cycle—in Detail

When you first set up your tank, there will be no ammonia (NH_3) or nitrite (NO_2), in the water. (An exception would be if there is a pre-existing problem with your tap water.) Soon, though, this will change.

Just as we produce ammonia in our urine, fish produce ammonia, too. However, they excrete it to a much lesser extent in the urine. Instead, fish mostly excrete ammonia through respiration in the gills. No matter, the result is the same, which is that the ammonia ends up in the water. Ammonia also enters the water when heterotrophic bacteria break down uneaten food, dead plant leaves, feces, and other detritus in the tank. These bacteria are different from the nitrifying bacteria, which are the good-guy bacteria I've been discussing.

I don't think I have to tell you how toxic ammonia can be! *Nitrosomonas* are the helpful bacteria that break down ammonia. They convert the ammonia into nitrite, which is still toxic to your fish, though not as toxic as ammonia. In a new tank, the ammonia levels will typically rise for about seven days after you introduce the first batch of fish. By this time, the helpful *Nitrosomonas* bacteria will usually have increased their population to the point where they can break down the ammonia faster than it is produced. So, a week after introducing fish, you usually will see ammonia levels drop back to zero.

Now, remember that the ammonia is being converted to nitrite. So as the helpful bacteria get things under control and the ammonia levels drop, you will see a simultaneous increase in the nitrite levels of your tank. Nitrite levels will tend to rise for roughly another seven days, and then they, too, will drop. That's because by this time another group of helpful bacteria, the *Nitrobacter,* will have developed a big enough population to oxidize the nitrite faster than it is produced. The result is that nitrite levels will drop back to zero.

Still, as the nitrite levels decrease, you will see nitrate (NO_3) levels increase. Fortunately, nitrate is generally considered harmless to freshwater fish, except in very high quantities. Your regular partial water changes will keep nitrate from building up to toxic levels. Additionally, plants in your tank may use it as a nutrient.

Anyway, once you've seen the ammonia level rise and fall back to zero, and then see the nitrite level rise and fall back to zero, your tank will be cycled. It should be safe to add the rest of your fish. Be aware that, when you do, you may see some temporary spikes in those ammonia and nitrite levels again, because you have increased the bioload in your tank and it takes the bacteria some time to increase their population to adjust to that.

The Timetable

Again, every tank is different, so the timetable will be different, too. The numbers I use in the following list are typical for tanks that I set up, but your results may vary.

Let me stress that the timetable I'm giving you is only a guideline. Only the actual running of ammonia and nitrite tests can tell you what stage your tank is at in the cycle, and when it is safe to add more fish. Do not ignore your test results because you want something else to be true.

If you are careful, you probably will see the following:

➤ No ammonia or nitrite will be present until after you introduce the fish. (The clock doesn't start ticking until you add the fish.)

➤ Once fish are added, ammonia will climb for approximately seven days. Then it will fall back to zero over a day or two.

➤ As ammonia falls, nitrite will climb for approximately the next seven days. Then it, too, will fall back to undetectable levels.

➤ As nitrite falls, nitrate will increase. Note, however, that I normally consider it a waste of time to test nitrate levels, unless you are having problems and no other cause can be found.

Corrective Action

When cycling a new tank, it's a good idea to run your water tests for ammonia and nitrite every day until the cycle is complete. Then, you can drop back to testing every week or two. What should you do if you find that ammonia or nitrite levels are elevated?

Fish and Tips

Many dealers offer a water testing service that is either free or inexpensive. Feel free to make use of this service, but I still recommend that you buy your own test kits to keep at home. Even if you use your own kits, your dealer can help you interpret the results of the tests.

The answer that is usually best may surprise you. That answer is: Do nothing. That's right, do nothing—but only if you aren't experiencing any problems with your fish. If they all appear healthy, if none are dying, then leave well enough alone. As the tank continues to cycle, Mother Nature will fix those ammonia and nitrite problems all by herself. On the other hand, if you are losing fish, or if the fish look overly stressed, corrective action may be necessary.

Moaning About Ammonia

So, what can you do if your ammonia level is high and the fish are having problems? Here are some possible solutions that you can mix or match:

➤ Add some ammonia-removing chips to your outside power filter. This stuff looks like white gravel and is a naturally occurring substance called zeolite. It will remove some ammonia, and then you can throw it away.

➤ Add one of those dormant bacteria products to break down the ammonia quickly. Note that some may cloud the water temporarily.

➤ Lower the pH slightly, perhaps to 6.8. I will talk about this more in the next chapter, but for now be aware that ammonia is more toxic in alkaline water. Lowering the pH below 7.0 will make the water acidic. Do not lower it too far, though, or you will create other problems. The ammonia will become the less toxic ammonium in slightly acidic water, and so it may not bother the fish at all. Eventually, the cycle will remove it.

➤ Change some water. Partial water changes will remove some ammonia. Keep in mind, though, that tap water is alkaline in most areas of the country. So you need to monitor the pH to avoid making the remaining ammonia more toxic.

➤ Add Amquel. This is a product that neutralizes the toxicity of ammonia. There are also some lower-quality copies of it on the market. If it neutralizes ammonia, why did I save this option for last? Wouldn't it be the best choice? Well, the answer is probably a resounding yes. It works great, but I'm reluctant to recommend it because I've just seen too many people misuse it.

As a dealer, I find myself wasting lots of time helping people figure out that they really don't have an ammonia problem, all because they used Amquel and didn't read the directions! To use Amquel properly, you need a compatible ammonia test kit. Not all ammonia test kits can be used with it. The salicylate-based kits must be used with it, while the Nessler's Reagent-based kits cannot be, because they give false-positive readings when used with Amquel. In other words, you will think you have ammonia when you don't. So you will add more Amquel, which will make you think your ammonia has gone up even more, which will make you panic.

When Nitrite Isn't Right

What if the nitrite level is high and the fish are dying or looking stressed? What do you do, then?

➤ If you haven't done it already, add one teaspoon of aquarium salt per gallon of aquarium water. Salt doesn't remove the nitrite, but it makes it much less toxic to the fish. It also helps prevent some diseases. This probably is the only thing that you need to do if you're worried about high nitrite levels.

➤ Do a partial water change. This will dilute the nitrite.

➤ Try one of the dormant bacteria products. Some claim to reduce nitrites as well as ammonia, though I have serious doubts.

New Tank Syndrome

Here is a term that you will occasionally hear bandied about. Sometimes new tank syndrome refers to ammonia and nitrite levels and the cycling of new tanks. Sometimes it is used to describe cloudy water problems that often appear in newly set up tanks. Since I've already talked about ammonia and nitrite, let's just look at the cloudy water aspect of new tank syndrome. Basically, two things cause cloudy water: suspended particulates and suspended bacteria.

A brand-new, sparkling clean aquarium filter is not as efficient as an established one. The established filter is apt to be partially clogged, thereby allowing it to filter even finer particles. It will also have stickier filter media—since a bacterial slime will inhabit it. So a new filter is apt to let more particulates get through.

Until your aquarium cycles, there will not be a biological balance of bacteria in the system. Sometimes other bacteria in the water column will supermultiply, feeding on available nutrients. There are so many of them that they can give a cloudy appearance to the water. Note, however, that these are not the desired nitrifying bacteria. Those good-guy bacteria live on solid surfaces, not in the water column. Time will usually fix the problem, so be patient!

Chapter 11

Basic Water Chemistry

First off, let me state that I am not a chemist. I don't even play one on TV. I am a geek, though, so you know I won't be happy unless we talk about some technical stuff. That's what this chapter is all about. The topics are important, however, and I will do my best to keep them light.

Pondering pH

pH (always spelled with a lowercase p and a capital H) is the measurement of acidity or alkalinity. According to

Webster's Dictionary, the term pH comes from the French *pouvoir hydrogene,* which means "hydrogen power." It is a measurement of hydrogen ions. We measure pH on a scale from 0 to 14.0, with a pH of 7.0 being neutral. A pH of less than 7.0 is acid, and a pH above 7.0 is alkaline (or basic). The lower the pH, the more acid. The higher the pH, the more alkaline (or basic) we consider a sample to be.

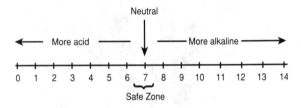

pH is measured on a scale of 0 to 14.0, with 7.0 being neutral. Low pH is acid. High pH is alkaline.

Additionally, pH is measured on a logarithmic scale, which means that each numerical change in pH actually represents a 10-fold change. That is, a pH of 7.0 is 10 times more alkaline than a pH of 6.0. And a pH of 6.0 is 100 times more acidic than a pH of 8.0. Don't concern yourself too much with that detail. The main thing to remember is that a one-point change in pH is a pretty big change, and a two-point change is a huge change. It is dangerous to change the pH of your aquarium too rapidly—either up or down.

What should the pH of your tank be? That may depend on what species you plan to keep. Livebearers, for example, prefer water that is harder and with a slightly alkaline pH, say around 7.4. Most African cichlids also prefer hard, alkaline water, with a pH around 7.8. In the wild, many tetras come from areas where the pH is in the low sixes.

Most fish, no matter where they come from, can tolerate a pH between 6.5 and 7.5. In fact, if you keep your tank's pH around the neutral point of 7.0, there isn't a fish around that won't do well in it. A pH of 7.0 is as ideal as you can get for the broadest mix of species.

Assessing Acidity

How do you know what your pH is? Simple—you test it. There are many kits on the market that are cheap and easy to use. The basic procedure is to fill a vial with water from the aquarium, add a few drops of the reagent, and then compare the color to a color chart to get your numerical reading. Some kits use powdered reagents. You may still run across pH tape, which is a test kit that uses strips of litmus paper that change color when you dunk them in the tank. Litmus paper test kits are much less accurate.

Fish and Tips

Follow your test kit's directions carefully. Some kits require you to view through the side of the vial to determine the color, and some require you to view down through the top of the vial. Improper viewing will distort the reading.

It is a good idea to measure the pH of your tap water so that you have a baseline. However, don't measure it directly out of the tap, as you probably won't get an accurate reading. Tap water has been stored under pressure in your water system, and will have extra gases dissolved in it. Coming from underground, tap water also may be devoid of some necessary gases. Some gases affect the pH. So aerate the sample—put it in a jar and shake it for a couple of minutes—before testing. This will drive out excess gases, allow regular atmospheric gases to be absorbed, and result in a more accurate reading. There is no need to aerate samples taken from the aquarium for testing. Your filter has already aerated the water for you.

My pH Has pHallen and It Can't Get Up

One thing you will find with regular testing is that the pH of your tank probably will not be stable over time. Instead, it will tend to drop. How fast this happens will depend on how many natural buffers are in your tap water. You may find that the pH drops within days or weeks, or it may not appear to drop at all—unless you go a really long time without a water change.

Fish School

A *buffer* is a combination of an acid or base with a salt that, when in solution, tends to stabilize the pH of the solution.

Why does the pH tend to drop? The answer is biological activity. You will remember that bacteria convert ammonia to nitrite, and nitrite to nitrate. Well, a by-product of that process is the release of acids into the water. If your tap water is low in natural buffers, these acids will cause the pH to drop. If your tap water is high in natural buffers, it may take a long time for the acids to deplete them all, so you may not see the pH drop until you've gone a long time without a water change.

What else affects pH? Carbon dioxide forms carbonic acid when dissolved in water. So if your aeration is insufficient to drive off excess carbon dioxide, the CO_2 can build up and cause the pH to fall slightly.

Photosynthesis also affects pH. Plants use CO_2 when they photosynthesize. That means that during the day they will pull CO_2 from the water, resulting in less formation of carbonic acid. So the pH will rise slightly during the day. At night, plants respire and the pH will fall a bit.

Salt affects pH—sometimes. It depends on the kind of salt. When you buy aquarium salt, which is straight sodium chloride, it should have absolutely no effect on pH or hardness. Sea salt, however, is another story. It contains other minerals that will increase the hardness and pH of the water. African cichlid salts do the same.

Okay, I've talked about some things that affect pH. Now, let's talk about things that are affected *by* pH.

Ammonia and pH

The most important thing that pH affects is the toxicity of ammonia. Ammonia (NH_3), excreted by the fish, is much more toxic in alkaline water. In acid water, it ionizes into the less toxic ammonium (NH_{4+}). So the higher the pH in your tank, the more dangerous will be any existing ammonia.

Interestingly, if your pH falls below 6.4 or so, the helpful bacteria that break down ammonia will start failing and the ammonium levels will climb. Fortunately, since the pH is low, the less toxic ammonium may not bother the fish much. However, do you see the danger here? What happens if something makes the pH go up? That's right. The ammonium becomes the very toxic ammonia.

Altering pH

First, I want to emphasize that it is usually best not to mess with your aquarium's pH. If your tank normally stays within that 6.5 to 7.5 range, it is probably best not to fiddle with the pH to try to make it "perfect." My recommendation is to only mess with the pH when you're having problems that seem attributed directly to it. Remember that a one-point change in pH is really a 10-fold change. So fiddling with the pH is sometimes much rougher on the fish than letting them adapt to what is normal for the local water conditions.

When adding chemicals to alter the pH, always start out with less than you think you'll need, and add from there. Once added, you can't remove the stuff without changing water. It may be helpful to put some aquarium water in a bucket, add a measured amount of adjusting chemical to it, and then test to see how much change it made. You can then prorate the measurement to dose the whole tank.

Bumping the pH Up

It is usually fairly easy to increase the pH. Here are some ways to do it:

➤ Change some water. This is the best choice for most of you. Usually, when your pH is low it is because you are not changing enough water. Remember that pH tends to drop over time, due to biological activity in the tank. Water changes are usually the best way to bring the pH up, because tap water is usually alkaline. However, if you live in an area where it isn't, look at the next possibilities.

➤ Add a little sodium bicarbonate (baking soda) to the tank. This will bring up your pH, but be careful not to add too much at once. Test your pH to get a baseline, then add perhaps one-eighth teaspoon of sodium bicarbonate per 10 gallons, and test the water again to see how much change it made. Proceed from there. It is best not to change the pH by more than one-half point per day, to prevent shock to the fish.

➤ Mix some dolomite or crushed coral (gravels normally sold for saltwater tanks) into your substrate.

These calcareous gravels will increase the pH and water hardness in the tank. Unfortunately, I can't tell you how much to add because every tank is different. Perhaps you could try adding a pound or two per 10 gallons, and then give it a few days before you decide if you need more. Too much will raise your pH higher than you probably want it to go.

➤ Add a decorative calcareous rock or two. Most of the whitish or light-colored soft rocks available at the pet store will fit this category. Your dealer can point them out. The advantage of this method over the calcareous gravel is that the rocks are easier to remove if you decide they aren't working the way you want.

➤ Try one of the other chemicals sold. There are some tablets available that contain a mix of buffers designed to achieve a designated pH. They may be designed to achieve 6.5, 7.0, 7.2, and so on.

Knocking the pH Down

Lowering the pH is usually much more difficult. Depending on the amount of naturally occurring buffers in your water, the chemicals that you add to acidify a tank may be quickly neutralized. It is not uncommon to test the next day and see that the pH has returned to its original level. I'll talk about buffers more in a bit. Here are some ways to lower pH:

➤ Use sodium biphosphate powder, available at your aquarium store. Follow the directions I gave above for sodium bicarbonate.

➤ Try one of the other pH-reducing chemicals available. There are liquids and also buffer tablets that target a designated pH, as mentioned previously.

➤ Add some peat to your filter box. Peat lowers both pH and hardness, but it can be tricky to use. I generally steer people away from this method. For starters, not all types of peat are safe—the stuff sold in aquarium stores should be, though. Also, there are different grades of it, so it's hard to say how much to use. Peat also releases some organic matter along with the acids, and that's not particularly good. Peat may turn your water an ugly brown.

Dissolved Oxygen

Obviously, your fish need to breathe oxygen to live. Since most fish take their oxygen directly from the water via gills, you must be sure that there is enough dissolved oxygen in the water to sustain them. There are test kits that measure the level of dissolved oxygen (DO), but you normally don't need to concern yourself with them. Instead, merely note the behavior of your fish to be sure that they aren't gasping, and regularly verify that your aeration and filtration is adequately circulating the water.

Fish and Tips

Many people mistakenly think that the bubbles from the aerators add oxygen. It is easy to see why they think so. However, experiments have shown that the bubbles add practically no oxygen to the water. Rather, their job is to circulate the water past the top surface, where the carbon dioxide can be exchanged for oxygen.

Many of you may be thinking that photosynthesis plays a big role in the oxygenation of your aquarium. You learned in biology class about how plants take in carbon dioxide that the animals have excreted, and through photosynthesis, release oxygen (O_2) back into the environment.

That does happen, but unless your aquarium has no aeration or filtration to circulate the water, photosynthesis has little effect on the tank.

While it is true that plants can convert carbon dioxide to oxygen, they only do it when the light is strong enough for them to photosynthesize. At night, plants respire. That is, they use oxygen—just like animals. So in a heavily planted tank with no circulation, dissolved oxygen levels can dip drastically at night. The result is that you can't count on the plants to keep sufficient oxygen levels.

The real exchange of CO_2 for oxygen takes place at the surface of your water. It is the circulation of the water that aerates your tank. Circulation takes the carbon dioxide–laden water from down below and carries it to the surface, where the CO_2 can escape and new oxygen can be absorbed. Without circulation, your tank becomes stagnant and has trouble making this gas exchange.

Carbon Dioxide

Carbon dioxide is excreted by your fish. This compound probably has the most extensive effect in your aquarium, because it affects so many things. Obviously, if the carbon dioxide level is too high or the oxygen level too low, your fish will suffocate. Carbon dioxide is a source of nutrition for plants, as well. It also plays many other roles.

Dissolved CO_2 is the key ingredient in the *carbonate system* of your aquarium. The carbonate system is a complex interaction of CO_2 that affects both the general hardness and carbonate hardness of the water in your aquarium. Let me say that this relationship is so complicated and dynamic that even I have trouble understanding it. So I'll just list a few key points that you may find interesting:

➤ In acid water (pH below 6.0), dissolved carbon dioxide exists mainly as free CO_2.

➤ In neutral or slightly alkaline water (pH 7.0 to 8.0), dissolved carbon dioxide is mostly found in the form of bicarbonates.

➤ In highly alkaline water (pH over 10), dissolved CO_2 exists largely in the form of carbonates.

➤ Carbonates and bicarbonates influence the carbonate hardness of the water.

➤ Carbonates can combine with calcium to fall out of solution as calcium carbonate, lowering both general and carbonate hardness.

➤ Additionally, carbon dioxide can lower the pH and the resulting acids redissolve calcium carbonates, increasing both general and carbonate hardness.

The result is that carbon dioxide has a relationship with the pH, the carbonate hardness, and even the general hardness. CO_2 is busy stuff! There are test kits available, if you are curious about your tank's CO_2 level. But generally, this stuff gets so complex that I wouldn't mess with it unless you suspect a problem.

Hydrogen Sulfide

Once you start your filter systems, you should never turn them off, except to do maintenance. The helpful bacteria in your tank need oxygen to do their job. They are aerobic bacteria. If you turn off the filters, especially with undergravel filters, the water won't circulate enough to get the oxygen where it needs to be. So the good-guy bacteria die off. In their place, anaerobic bacteria develop. They break down waste, too, but they do it in a manner that produces toxic hydrogen sulfide gas as a by-product. Hydrogen sulfide is the gas that makes rotten eggs smell.

Chapter 12

Water Changes and Filter Maintenance

In This Chapter

➤ The importance of water changes

➤ How to use a gravel vacuum

➤ Conditioning tap water

➤ Dealing with evaporation

➤ How to clean and maintain your filter

Your fish are swimming in their own toilet. It is your job to flush it for them! Regular partial water changes are *extremely* important to your fish.

Partial water changes have two main purposes:

1. They remove dissolved waste. (If you use a gravel vacuum to perform this chore, you also will remove solid waste.)

2. They replace depleted trace elements.

Partial water changes have other incidental benefits, too. Your fish will show better colors. They will grow faster. They will be more disease resistant. If you want your fish to breed, you will also have better success.

Time for a Change

For most tanks a good rule to follow is to change 25 percent of the aquarium water every two weeks. That is enough to keep the typical aquarium in healthy condition. However, be sure to consider the bioload in your tank. If you are keeping large fish, or if your tank is crowded, you may need to change more water, more often, to keep the water quality in good condition.

Fish and Tips

Evaporation doesn't count! Your partial water changes should be made in addition to replacing any water that evaporates.

Your test kits can help you judge if you are changing enough water. If you find that the pH is falling, for example, you may not be changing enough water. Test kits are very helpful for finding problems. They are also very helpful for monitoring trends.

While your test kits can tell you when you are *not* changing enough water, they cannot tell you when you *are* changing enough. In other words, don't let good readings fool you into thinking that you can skip regular partial water changes. You can test only a very limited number of water-quality parameters. There are many other things that you cannot test, and regular partial water changes provide assurance that you are dealing with those things, too.

The Price of Procrastination

What happens if you don't keep up with your regular partial water changes? It depends. If you miss one occasionally, it is probably no big deal. If you miss them often, it gets more dangerous. How dangerous depends on the bioload in your tank and the natural buffering capacity of your local tap water. You probably recall from Chapter 11 on water chemistry that as waste builds up and biological filtration occurs, acids are produced. Over time, the pH in the aquarium falls. You also may recall that if the pH falls low enough, the helpful bacteria in the tank will stop breaking down ammonia, so ammonia levels climb. Fortunately, ammonia is much less toxic in acid water. So the fish (being hardy creatures) may survive the acid pH and high ammonia for some time without obvious detrimental effects.

However, if the owner of this low pH–high ammonia aquarium decides it is time to make that long overdue partial water change, what do you think will happen? Remember that tap water is usually alkaline. Let's say the owner, realizing that a water change is overdue, changes 50 percent, instead of the usual 25. That means 50 percent of the ammonia will remain after he refills the tank. Since the tap water is alkaline, it is going to raise the pH in the aquarium.

Remember that ammonia toxicity increases with pH. So, while this hobbyist removes 50 percent of the ammonia with the partial water change, by increasing the pH he makes the remaining 50 percent much more toxic. He stands a very good chance of seeing his fish suddenly go belly up.

Suck Muck? Yuck!

A gravel vacuum is your best friend when it comes to aquarium maintenance. This inexpensive muck-sucking device makes it very easy to clean gravel and change water, all at the same time. Some would even say that a gravel vacuum is fun to use. (I wouldn't say that, but some would.)

The gravel vacuum is a simple device, consisting of a large-diameter tube attached to the end of a siphon hose. You use it to siphon water from your tank. While siphoning, you poke the large tube into the gravel. The flow of water through the large tube is fast enough to tumble the gravel and rinse out the detritus, but not fast enough to siphon out the gravel, too.

With a little practice, you probably will be able to clean the entire gravel bed with your gravel vacuum during each 25 percent water change. If you can't cover the entire bottom while siphoning the allotted amount of water, don't worry. Just take up where you left off at the next water change. Or, if you like, change a bit more than 25 percent.

Starting a Siphon

Gravel vacuums work by siphoning water. That is, simple gravity causes water to run down through a hose to a lower level. There are no motors or moving parts. The hose acts a bit like the spout on a watering can.

There are several easy ways to start a gravel vacuum. I use the quickest way. I place the large tube in the tank. I use my mouth to give a quick suck on the hose end of the device, and then quickly flick that end of the hose down into a bucket before water comes out. If you do it right, you can start the siphon without ever getting a drop of fish water in your mouth. However, fish water doesn't taste any different from regular water, if you ask me.

Cleaning the Gravel

Once you have the siphon started and water is flowing into the bucket, merely poke the large tube deep into your gravel, then lift. When you lift, the water will flow up through the gravel in the tube, washing away any detritus. The gravel, being heavier, will tumble back into the tank. Continue the poke and lift method until you've removed the amount of water intended for replacement.

The smaller your particles of gravel, the higher they will rise inside the tube of the gravel vacuum. If they start getting too close to the hose—close enough to where they might siphon out—just place your thumb over the end of the hose to reduce or pause the flow. With a little practice, you can master the technique of lightly pinching or releasing the end of the hose to increase or decrease the flow.

Once you finish, discard the dirty water that you collected in the bucket. You may be surprised at how much crud you pull out of a tank! Another great thing about gravel vacuums is that they remove all that crud without stirring up things in the tank. You can use the same bucket (after you've rinsed it) to draw water to refill your tank. Make sure the new water is within 2°F (1°C) of the existing water, so that there is no temperature shock to the fish.

Something's Fishy

Be careful not to suck up any fish while gravel vacuuming. Usually the fish are smart enough to stay away, but not always. Plus, they sometimes rush over thinking that the particles of tumbling gravel are bits of food. If a fish does enter the vacuum tube, simply place your thumb over the output hose to stop the flow until the fish swims back out.

Be a Quick-Change Artist

Many hobbyists put off changing their water because they think it is too much work. It shouldn't be. If you know the right way to make a partial water change, you can do it quickly. Of course, like anything else, practice makes perfect. So you may not be able to achieve maximum speed on your first try.

It should only take five minutes to make a partial water change in a typical 20-gallon aquarium. I picked this size tank because it is typical, and because a 25 percent water change fits nicely in a single five-gallon bucket.

Gather Your Supplies

You need the following items:

- ✓ Gravel vacuum
- ✓ Five-gallon fish bucket
- ✓ Dechlorinating water conditioner
- ✓ Optional: A teaspoon to measure out the water conditioner, if it is not a drops-per-gallon brand
- ✓ Thermometer
- ✓ Optional: Saucer (the thing you put under your coffee cup)

Remove the Old Water

Set the bucket on the floor beneath your tank. Use your gravel vacuum to siphon water into the bucket, removing as much debris from the gravel bed as possible. When the bucket is full, carry it somewhere to be dumped—perhaps to a sink or toilet.

Collect Fresh Water

Rinse the bucket and refill with water of the correct temperature. I have been doing this for so long that I can tell the temperature of the water merely by touching it, but you probably will need to use a thermometer. The new water should be within a couple of degrees of the existing tank water.

Refill the Tank

To refill the tank, lift the bucket of new water and pour it slowly into the tank. I pour it onto a large rock or piece of driftwood to keep it from disturbing the gravel. You may need to place a saucer on the bottom of the tank and pour onto that, to keep from disturbing the gravel. Also, if the bucket is too heavy for you, you will either need a smaller container to dip water, or perhaps you can use a small powerhead or water pump.

With a little practice, you can accomplish all the above in around five minutes or so. It's quick. It's easy. More important, you never have to move the fish or tear down your tank to clean it.

Conditioning Tap Water

One thing to remember as I talk about this topic is that we don't all live in the same place. (Thank goodness! My apartment is too crowded already.) Your local tap water may be very different from mine. It may be harder, softer, more acidic, or more alkaline. You may have lots of iron or none at all. You may buy your water from the city, or you may have your own well. Run-off from fertilizers on farms may give you high levels of nitrates, pesticides, and other nasty stuff in your water.

Conditions vary everywhere, so it is impossible for me to put in this book a simple recipe for conditioning tap water that will work for everyone. Besides running your own water tests, you may want to ask your dealer what he knows about the local water quality. You may even want to call the local water department to see what they can tell you. In addition to the advice I am about to present, you also may need to review Chapter 11 on water chemistry for information on how to deal with your tap water.

The one thing that almost all of you will need is a good dechlorinator. Unless you draw your water from your own well, you probably have chlorinated tap water. The simplest dechlorinators are solutions of sodium thiosulfate. You add it to the tank, and it instantly neutralizes the chlorine. These days, most water conditioners include ingredients that do other tasks, too.

Chlorine and Chloramines

Chlorine is added to the water in municipal water supplies to kill microscopic organisms. It does its job well, but if you have ever been swimming in a chlorinated swimming pool, you know that chlorine also is rough on mucous membranes, such as the eyes and nose. It does the same thing to fish, but they have an added disadvantage. Their gills are exposed to the chlorinated water, and chlorine damages gills.

So you need to remove chlorine from the tap water. The easiest way to do so is to purchase and use one of the many commercial tap water conditioners. Your dealer will carry many brands, all inexpensive. To remove chlorine, you dose the product in drops per gallon or teaspoons per 10 gallons, depending on the brand. It's quick and easy.

Something's Fishy

Not all products are created equal. Many products that claim to neutralize chloramine really only handle the chlorine part of the compound. They release the ammonia and do nothing to neutralize it.

In a few areas around the country, the local water supplies have high levels of dissolved organic matter. Chlorine can combine with these to form carcinogenic substances (trihalomethanes). To prevent that, some municipal water supplies add both chlorine and ammonia to the water. These two combine into new compounds called chloramines. Chloramines also disinfect water, but don't combine with organic matter.

Your dechlorinating water conditioner will neutralize both chlorine and chloramines. However, when chloramines are neutralized, the ammonia is released! We know how dangerous ammonia is to fish. If you have a well-established tank, it probably will not be a big deal. Your biological filtration will quickly neutralize the ammonia. In a new, uncycled tank, though, the ammonia could be especially deadly.

Ask your dealer if your local tap water contains chloramines. If it does, you may want to consider adding some zeolite ammo-chips to remove the ammonia, or dechlorinating your water with a product that will neutralize the ammonia, too. Of those, Amquel is the only one that I recommend.

Aquarium Salt

Many dealers and hobbyists add a bit of aquarium salt to their tanks. Salt can help prevent disease, and some fish just plain do better if there is a bit of salt in the water. There are many formulas to decide how much salt to add, but most will use one teaspoon of salt per gallon of aquarium water. That's 10 teaspoons in a 10-gallon tank, and 55 teaspoons in a 55-gallon tank. (You may want to remember that a cup is 48 teaspoons, to save yourself some measuring!)

Adding one teaspoon of salt per gallon is often recommended. You may want to add more with certain species,

mollies for example. There is not one species of freshwater
fish that will be bothered by two teaspoons of salt per
gallon.

Fish School

Aquarium salt is pure, uniodized sodium chloride. Don't
confuse it with sea salt, which has many other ingredients.

Is it necessary to add salt to your tank? Probably not. You
may want to see how things work without adding the salt.
If the tank does just fine, and it very well may, then don't
bother adding salt. If you find livebearers getting clamped
fins and shimmies, then you probably need to get some
salt in there quickly. Some say salt is rough on plants, but
I've kept plants in two teaspoons of salt per gallon and
not noticed any problems.

Vitamins and Trace Elements

There are products available whose purpose is to add vitamins and trace elements to the water to make your tank
healthier. Frankly, I think those products are a waste of
money. Dumping that stuff in the water does little, if anything, for your fish, because fish really don't drink much
water. What it does is feed the algae in your tank. If you
want more algae, then maybe adding vitamins and trace
elements is a good idea. If you think your plants aren't
getting enough nutrients, then buy proper fertilizers.

Gas Saturation

When water is under pressure in your tap, it can absorb
more gases. Have you ever drawn a glass of water and

noticed that it was cloudy for a minute? Jillions of tiny bubbles eventually float to the top and the water clears. When you fill your aquarium the first time, you may find a layer of bubbles coating the glass after a few minutes. These bubbles are the result of gas saturation.

Here's the problem. If you place fish into water that is still supersaturated with gases, it is very rough on the fish. These gases may be absorbed into the bloodstream and condense out of solution there. Bubbles build up in the bloodstream and may kill the fish! It's the same kind of situation as when deep sea divers surface too fast and get the bends. When they were deep underwater, they were also under high pressure. More gases were absorbed into their blood. If the diver surfaces too fast, the gases condense into bubbles in their bloodstream. It's very painful and can be fatal.

To prevent gas saturation problems, all you have to do is aerate your water. The first time you fill your tank, it's not a big deal because the filters will aerate the water—driving out excess gases and ensuring that ample supplies of needed ones are present. However, it is always best to play it safe. Agitate your tap water as you draw it. Are you drawing into a bucket? Set the stream so that a real turmoil results. This will drive off excess gases. If you use a hose to fill a tank, put your finger over the end to make the spray jet out hard, and then spray it against your hand, instead of spraying directly into the tank. This will agitate the water quite well.

Vanishing Into Thin Air

A certain amount of evaporation will occur in every aquarium. How fast it happens will depend on several factors, including the humidity of the air in the room, water temperature, whether the tank is covered or open, and how much circulation occurs at the water surface.

Evaporation is only a problem if you let it go too far. Your tank could eventually go dry! Of course, your fish probably would be dead from neglect long before that happened.

Probably the most important thing you need to know about evaporation is that, when it occurs, only the water leaves. The dissolved waste and minerals remain behind. You will remember that a 25 percent partial water change should be made every two weeks. What if your tank evaporates by 25 percent every two weeks? Is it okay just to top it off with new water? No!

It is not okay because the new water adds more minerals without removing any of the old ones or removing any dissolved waste. If you repeatedly top off a tank without removing any water, the waste and minerals will continue to build up. So when you make your regular partial water changes, make them *in addition* to topping off evaporation.

Filter Maintenance

Your filter cleans the tank. You clean the filter. Filters don't remove waste from the system, they only separate it. It is your job to remove the waste. Usually, you do so by replacing filter media, but sometimes you rinse and reuse the media. Following are some common types of filters and typical methods for cleaning them.

Undergravel Filters

Undergravel filters are the easiest and least expensive to maintain. The gravel functions as the filter media, and you clean it with a gravel vacuum when you make your partial water changes. Since you have to siphon water to make your partial water change anyway, using a gravel vacuum is no extra work at all. There is no filter media to change. However, don't forget to replace your airstones as needed.

Use the gravel vacuum to clean around plants and rocks, removing as much debris from the gravel as possible. If you draw out the allotted amount of water before you clean the whole bottom, don't worry about it. Just take up where you left off at the next water change.

Outside Power Filters

There are many brands of outside power filters. Most use special filter media that won't fit other filters. However, there are two basic categories of outside power filters. One group uses replaceable, slide-in filter cartridges. Others have reusable sponge filter media.

All outside power filters have magnetic impellers. Don't forget to remove the impeller occasionally and take a small filter brush to clean inside the impeller-well. If slime builds up in there, the filter can stop. Be careful not to get sand in the well. You also may need to use a filter brush to clean inside intake tubes and strainers.

Cartridge filter media. Cartridge filters are designed to be easy to clean. You slide out the dirty filter cartridge and pop in a new, clean one. It doesn't get much easier than that. Still, there is a disadvantage to that ease of use. When you throw away your filter media, you also throw away the helpful bacteria that colonized the media. So you temporarily reduce the biological filtration capacity of your tank.

There are a couple of things you can do to help, though. Large outside power filters may have two cartridges, instead of one. If so, it is better to change them on a rotating basis, instead of replacing both cartridges at once. That way, you retain the helpful bacteria on one cartridge, while the other recolonizes. If you use the refillable cartridges, you may want to replace the outer polyester media one time, and the activated carbon the next. Rotating the two types of media retains helpful bacteria. It's a bit of a pain to do, though, and definitely not as easy as tossing out one cartridge and popping in another.

Sponge filter media. One very popular brand uses a separate filter sponge and a bag of activated carbon. When the sponge gets dirty, you rinse it and reuse it . . . forever. Rinse the sponge with water that is close to aquarium temperature, so that you don't kill the helpful bacteria living on the sponge. You want to rinse out the debris, not sterilize the sponge.

The bags of activated carbon should be replaced at least monthly. Activated carbon can only adsorb so much waste and then it is no good. Worse, if you don't change your activated carbon often enough, and your pH drops, substances may be released back into the water.

You can buy pre-sized bags of activated carbon to fit your model of filter, or you can buy net filter bags and bulk activated carbon and bag your own. If you buy bulk carbon, get the good stuff. The price will usually reflect the quality. Good activated carbon will have a dull luster and relatively rough finish. Avoid the cheap, glassy black filter carbons. They are nothing more than crushed coal and are close to worthless. There are some excellent brands of activated carbon that come in pellet form. I highly recommend those.

Canister Filters

There are several brands of these. Follow the manufacturer's instructions for advice on disassembly and for recommendations on getting the best performance. When cleaning filter media, you should also take time to clean the impeller assembly and make sure that intake and output valves are not clogged with plant stems and leaves.

> ➤ **Filter compartments.** My favorite canister filters have separate plastic compartments inside. One uses ceramic noodle filter media, another holds activated carbon, and a third holds a filter sponge. At cleaning time, the ceramic noodles and sponge get rinsed and

reused forever. The activated carbon should be replaced at each filter change.

➤ **Filter sleeves.** Some brands have a central core around which you wrap a replaceable filter sleeve. One type of sleeve is soft polyester, another resembles an oil filter for a car. The type that looks like an oil filter will filter finer particles. Both types should be replaced when dirty.

➤ **Open design.** At least one brand of canister filter has a single large compartment for filter media. There are several types that can be used, all having unpronounceable German names. Follow the manufacturer's recommendations for best results.

Other Filters

What about maintenance on other types of filters?

➤ **Box or corner filters.** When the polyester media gets dirty, replace it. Replace the activated carbon at least monthly. If you have a model that uses an airstone, be sure to replace it when the flow slows, or you'll damage your air pump.

➤ **Internal cartridge filters.** Replace the cartridge at least monthly.

➤ **Sponge filters.** Rinse them with water that is close to aquarium temperature. The sponge should last a long, long time. If you see the sponge starting to collapse, or notice reduced output, it is a sign that the sponge needs cleaning. Depending on the bioload in your tank, you may need to do it weekly, biweekly, or monthly.

➤ **Powerheads.** Though not really filters, they power many filters. Keep an eye to be sure that the intake strainers don't become clogged. Sometimes you will need to disassemble the powerhead to remove the crud that gets inside.

Chapter 13

Foods and Feeding

In This Chapter

➤ Find a balanced diet for your fish

➤ Learn how much to offer at mealtimes

➤ Discover delicious dinners and tasty snacks

➤ Vacation foods and electronic fish feeders

You will enjoy watching your fish for many reasons. Ornamental fish are relaxing and beautiful to watch. But I bet you will soon discover that you enjoy your aquarium the very most when you are feeding the fish. That's because it's a time when you can truly interact with the inhabitants of your tank.

Your fish will soon learn that their meals come from *you*, so they will be flocking to the front of the tank whenever you come near. Yes, your fish will learn to recognize you. If several people regularly feed the fish, they may come rushing forward to greet any human that is nearby.

However, if you are their only caterer, you may be the only one who gets that excited response when you approach the tank. It'll make you feel loved.

Still, it is not just the attention of the fish you will enjoy at feeding time. You also will get a major kick out of watching the little critters eat. I love watching tetras flash to the surface to grab a flake of food, before shooting back down below as if avoiding some imaginary predator. And it is comical to hear the little tiger barbs, with their poor manners, noisily snapping up food at the surface.

Fishin' for Nutrition

Nutrition is a cornerstone of successful fishkeeping. You can do everything else right, but if you don't offer the proper types of food and in sufficient quantities, your fish will not survive for long. Most of the species available will take flake foods quite readily, but others may require live foods to survive.

It is your responsibility to find out what diet is required by the species you want to buy, *before* you purchase them. A good dealer will alert you if you choose a species with specialized dietary requirements, but you can't necessarily count on that happening.

Many prepared fish foods on your dealer's shelves will provide a well-balanced diet for most species, all by themselves. However, there is no one food that will be perfect for all fish. Some species prefer more animal matter in their diet. Others prefer more plant-based foods. So if you offer only one food, although all will eat it, the food may be balanced for only a few of the species in your tank.

The Spice of Life

When customers ask me what is the best food for their fish, I always give them the same answer. "Variety." Offering a variety of foods is absolutely the best way to go. It lets individual species pick the foods that best suit them. Besides, it gives everyone a chance to have a more stimulating diet.

My fish at home get a good selection of foods. I tend to keep about a half dozen or so varieties of dried foods around, including flakes, pellets, and freeze-dried foods. Also, there are always at least a couple of varieties of frozen foods in the freezer for them, and I occasionally bring home some live foods, too. Every meal is something different for the fish at my house. Ideally, it will be the same at yours.

An inexpensive way to offer a variety of foods, without buying several types at once, is to purchase one of the multi-packs available. There are cans of flakes that have four compartments and a special dispenser top that you turn to choose the flavor you want to offer at that meal. Recently, some frozen foods have become available in multi-flavor cube-packs, too.

Don't Stuff Them to the Gills

How often should you feed your fish? Usually twice a day is best. I like to feed my fish when I get up in the morning, and again in the evening when I come home from work. Work out a feeding schedule that fits your own schedule, and don't worry too much if you have to alter it occasionally. The fish won't complain . . . much. If they miss the occasional meal, don't try to make it up at the next feeding. A fish's stomach can only hold so much food at once. Extra food is going to go uneaten and pollute the tank.

Learning how much food to feed is sometimes difficult. People often say to offer just a pinch of food, but how much is a pinch? Your pinch may be quite a bit different from mine. It may consist of just a couple of flakes or a couple of hundred flakes. When you buy your first batch of fish, ask your dealer to show you how much to feed. Don't settle for him giving you a rule or saying "a pinch." Ask him to spread some food in his hand to show you how much is right.When feeding flakes, pellets, or other dry foods to your fish, do not sprinkle the food directly from the can into your tank. Instead, sprinkle first into the palm of your hand, and then sprinkle that into the tank. That way, if you accidentally sprinkle too much, you can take corrective action rather than having excess food pollute your tank.

My favorite rule of feeding is based on a time limit. Offer only what the fish can eat in three minutes. If there is any food *at all* at the end of that time, you have overfed them. Even better, offer what they will eat in 30 seconds to a minute. There are a couple of exceptions that are allowable here. For example, some pelleted foods for bottom dwellers may take more than three minutes to soften up enough to be eaten. That is fine, as long as the pellets are consumed in a reasonable time—say half an hour. Also, this rule applies to packaged foods. If you are feeding live foods, some of them may be able to escape or hide for longer than three minutes. Again, that is okay, if they are eaten within a reasonable time.

Fish and Tips

You can kill your fish by overfeeding, but it is not overeating that will kill them. Rather, it is the resulting pollution from uneaten food that causes problems. Remember that you are not just feeding the fish, you are feeding the tank.

Until you learn just how much to feed, be sure to err on the side of underfeeding. That is, offer a small quantity of food, and if the fish snap it up quickly, offer a little more. You can do that until you get a better idea of how much is safe to offer all at once. It is very important not to over-feed, *especially* in a new tank.

Flaky Choices

Most hobbyists start out with at least one variety of flake food. Flake foods contain an amalgamation of ingredients that were mixed into a porridge and then cooked and dried into thin sheets. These sheets are broken into bits and packaged. No doubt you are familiar with this type of food. Most people start out with a brand of flake *staple food*. Staple foods provide balanced nutrition for most kinds of fish.

Don't limit your fish to staple food. There are many other flake foods that can help you provide interest and better-balanced nutrition. There are flakes containing a high concentration of *Spirulina* algae to provide extra vegetable content to herbivorous fish, and there are flakes containing brine shrimp or other ingredients to treat the more carnivorous varieties of fish. Also popular are flakes containing natural color-enhancing ingredients. These foods can help bring out the colors in your fish, making them look their best. Growth flakes are available for small fish, and some varieties of food come in a large size flake, for feeding the bigger fish you keep.

Cold Facts About Freeze-Dried Foods

Unlike most dry foods, which are a mix of ingredients that include items fish would never eat in the wild, freeze-dried foods actually consist of preserved aquatic animals that fish would find in their natural environment.

Mosquito larvae, daphnia (a tiny crustacean), tubifex worms, various types of shrimp, and bloodworms (sometimes labeled as red mosquito larvae or red grubs) are commonly available. Once these freeze-dried foods soak up some water, they are very much like offering freshly killed foods. However, your fish probably will gobble them down before they get a chance to soak.

The Lowdown on Bottom Feeders

Some foods come in pellet or tablet form. Tablet foods are for bottom dwellers. They sink straight to the bottom, where scavengers can get at them. There are algae tablets for plecostomus and other algae-eating fish, there are staple tablets for all fish, and there is even a brand of tablet made largely from compressed freeze-dried foods.

Pelleted foods may be either sinking or floating varieties. Sometimes, both types are mixed in the same package. Choose according to which fish you want to feed. Floating pellets can help top dwellers get their fair share, while sinking pellets do the same for scavengers. Pellets are also a convenient way to feed large fish.

You will find pelleted foods available for any type of fish that eats dry prepared foods, but there is an especially good selection available for goldfish and koi, and for cichlids.

Fresh from the Freezer

Hopefully, your dealer will stock a large supply of frozen fish foods, too. These days, many dealers have glass-fronted display freezers, similar to those found in grocery stores. If the store is small, though, it may keep only a tiny selection of foods in the back-room freezer and require that you request them. Most stores carry frozen brine shrimp, which is the old standby. These days, there are many other frozen fish foods available, including glassworms (*Chaoborus* larvae), daphnia, tubifex worms, bloodworms, and mosquito larvae—and those are just the freshwater fish foods.

Frozen foods come either in flat-packs or cube-packs. Flat-packs are self-sealing plastic bags with a block of food frozen inside. To feed these foods, you can either break off a chunk and toss it in the tank, or squeeze some out the edge of the plastic wrapper and swirl it in the tank until a sufficient quantity melts free. Of course, if you toss in a chunk, you can still swirl it around to get bits to melt free to keep the more voracious feeders from hogging it.

Cube-packs offer even more convenience. They come in clear plastic flip-top trays that resemble miniature ice cube trays. They cost slightly more than flat-packs, but they are much simpler to use. You simply push on the back to pop out the number of cubes you need, much like popping cold medicine out of one of those foil packs, and then toss the cubes into the tank. The fish do the rest.

Now Appearing Live

Frozen foods are the next best thing to live foods, which are the best of all. Live foods not only offer the most natural, freshest ingredients, they also put on a show. If you want to see your fish have a good time, offer live foods. Your fish will go nuts for them.

Following are some live foods you can find in pet stores. Some are foods that almost all fish will eat. Others will be useful only if you have large carnivorous fish.

Blackworms

(*Limnodrilus* spp.) These are an excellent food for most small to medium fish. Blackworms are one to two inches long and as big around as a pencil lead. They are especially good for bottom dwellers, such as cory cats and spiny eels. Live blackworms typically sell by the portion, which may contain several hundred worms.

Store live blackworms in the refrigerator, and change their water every day or two. There is a device called a *worm keeper* that consists of a tray with a very fine mesh bottom that nests on top of a larger outer tray. You fill the lower tray with water, and when it is time to change water, lift the top tray. The water will sift out, leaving just the worms, and then you change the water in the bottom tray. Easy. If you buy small portions, you can just store them in the container in which they are sold.

There are several ways to feed live blackworms to your fish. One way is simply to toss some in the tank and watch the fish munch away. Another is to use a worm feeder. The worm feeder is an inverted, perforated plastic cone that floats at the surface. You put the worms inside, and as they poke their heads and tails out of the holes, the fish yank them out and eat them. The advantage of this method is that fewer worms will find their way into the gravel, where they can hide from the fish.

If you want to feed live blackworms to bottom feeders, you could just toss them in the tank, but the other fish may gobble most before they get to the bottom, and some will dig too deeply to get caught. I like to take a one-inch deep plastic condiment cup, put one-half inch of gravel in it, and then sink it in the gravel at the bottom of the tank. Then, when you put worms in the cup, they will dig into the half inch of gravel, where the other fish can't get to them. The bottom feeders, however, will still be able to root them out easily, and the cup keeps the worms from digging too deep for the bottom feeders to reach.

Tubifex Worms

These are very similar to blackworms, but more commonly seen. They have a more reddish color, and when disturbed, clump into mats so tight that you will have a bit of trouble tearing them apart.

Rumor has it that tubificid worms, including blackworms and tubifex, can be carriers of fish disease. These worms live in areas where the water has high organic matter, and can be found in the sludge where sewage enters streams. I do not give much credence to these rumors. I have personally offered regular feedings of blackworms, and occasionally tubifex, to my fish with no negative results. In fact, the opposite has happened. Many of my specimens have turned out to be the largest, most colorful that I've seen of the species anywhere. I also know many professional aquarists and fish farmers who use these foods regularly and swear by them.

Brine Shrimp

(*Artemia* spp.) Though these animals are not something your fish are likely to encounter in the wild, your fish will love them. Brine shrimp live in salt marshes, areas where the water is too salty for most fish. In fact, brine shrimp live in areas where the water may dry up, and they have evolved a unique way to survive this. Their dehydrated eggs can last for many years, hatching when the rains return. I have read accounts of thousand-year-old sediments that still held viable eggs. You also can buy brine shrimp eggs to hatch as food for your baby fish. Don't feed the eggs directly, though. The shells are not digestible.

Brine shrimp are sold by the portion, which may include several hundred of them. If you don't crowd them too much, you can keep brine shrimp at room temperature until fed to the fish. You also can refrigerate them. If you refrigerate brine shrimp, they will stop moving, but regain activity when rewarmed.

Glassworms

(*Chaoborus* larvae) These half-inch animals are an interesting food for your fish. They are the totally transparent larvae of a mosquito-like insect, but the adults don't suck blood. They are great for your fish, but they are predatory. So don't mix them with tiny baby fish. Glassworms should be refrigerated until use.

Earthworms
Various sizes and species of earthworms are sold as bait and fish food. They will be relished as a treat by fish large enough to eat them. Earthworms also can be diced into bits for smaller fish.

Mealworms
Commonly sold as food for reptiles and amphibians, mealworms are readily eaten by many fish as well. They drown very quickly, so if you are offering them to a fish that requires its food to be live, don't feed too many at once—or most will drown before they are eaten.

Crickets
Most pet shops and bait shops carry crickets. Assorted sizes are available, and they are relished by most fish that are large enough to eat them.

What to Do on Your Summer Vacation
One great thing about fish is that you can leave them unattended and without food for short periods of time. If you are going to be gone for a weekend, don't worry about them. They will be fine.

If you're going to be gone longer than two or three days, however, you must make arrangements for the care of your fish. If you have someone you trust—someone who knows how much to feed fish and how to watch for problems and take corrective action—you may want to use that person as a fish sitter while you are away. Come to think of it, it wouldn't hurt to have someone look in on the fish, even if you're just gone for the weekend.

Electronic fish feeders are another option. These are devices that clip on the top of the aquarium. You set the timer, and they dispense meals of dry foods to your fish. Some models automatically feed twice a day. Other models are fully programmable. Electronic fish feeders may seem a bit expensive, but remember that you don't only have to use them when you are on vacation. You can use them to feed dry foods to your fish 365 days per year, and supplement with live and frozen foods at will.

Fish and Tips

When using electronic fish feeders, make sure the flakes or pellets are small enough to fit through the dispenser opening, or it will clog. Also, do not pack food too tightly into the storage hopper, or the food can become compacted and will not be released.

For quick trips, consider using one of the "weekend foods" or "vacation foods" that are sold in the stores, *but only as a last resort.* These are plaster blocks that have food particles distributed within. When you toss one in the tank, the plaster slowly dissolves, exposing food for the fish to nibble at. Typically, you use one per 10 gallons.

However, these products are not good choices, for several reasons. First, there are many more chemicals in them than there is food. These chemicals are dissolving into your water, changing the water chemistry, and the rate of dissolution varies greatly, depending on the pH and hardness of the water in your tank. The little bit of food that is available is only going to be available to fish that are willing to feed off the bottom. Finally, there is a real question about how long the food stays fresh, once it hits the tank and gets wet. I often wonder if vacation food isn't rotten after the first day.

Chapter 14

Plants and the Wet Green Thumb

In This Chapter

➤ Lessons in lighting

➤ Facts about fertilizers

➤ Pointers on pruning

Plants make a tank come alive. They give a natural and more pleasing appearance to your aquarium. They make your fish more comfortable, too—providing places to hide, areas to explore, and sites for breeding. You want your fish to feel like they are at home, not in a bare jail cell.

Be Enlightened About Lighting

Intense, full-spectrum light is absolutely the most important factor in growing thick, lush plants. Without strong light, your plants will either die or grow into emaciated, spindly versions of their former selves.

Plants need light to photosynthesize. Unfortunately, the typical single-strip light and fluorescent full-hood provide enough light to see the fish, but they do not provide enough light for most species of plants to prosper. Without intense light, you will be greatly limited in the number of species of plants that you can keep alive.

When it comes to lighting, you must provide three things for maximum plant growth:

➤ Proper spectral color

➤ Sufficient duration

➤ Effective intensity

While almost any kind of light bulb, in sufficient quantity, will grow plants, some are much better at it than others. Full-spectrum light is the best. Full-spectrum bulbs contain a complete range of colors of the visible spectrum, and a bit of the invisible spectrum, too. Full-spectrum bulbs will give off light that appears white but may have accents in particular parts of the spectrum. Plants make particular use of red and blue wavelengths, so many full-spectrum bulbs have extra peaks in those colors.

Twelve hours of light per day works quite well. Anywhere from 10 to 14 hours of light per day is acceptable. Twenty-four hours of light will not help your plants, and may be detrimental. Like animals, plants have a daily metabolic rhythm. After a period of time, they quit photosynthesizing and rest, whether the lights are on or not.

It's Light or Death

There is no substitute for providing sufficient light intensity. You cannot take a bulb with poor spectral output and run it longer to get the proper effect. It just won't work. Be bright and buy bright lights!

So, how much light is needed? A good general rule of thumb is to use two to five watts of fluorescent light per gallon. I give a range because some species require more light than others and because taller tanks will require more light than shallow tanks. The farther light travels, the more spread out and less concentrated it becomes.

Using the two-to-five-watt-per-gallon rule, you can see that a 10-gallon tank would require 20 to 50 watts of light. Since this size aquarium is relatively shallow—only 12 inches tall—using the low end of that scale should work out just fine. In other words, at least 20 watts of light should be plenty.

Fish and Tips

To retain their color, reddish plants require the most light, and some also need extra iron fertilization.

According to the rule, a 55-gallon tank would require 110 to 275 watts of light. Since this tank is almost twice as tall as a 10-gallon, which means it will take almost four times as much light to reach the bottom with the same intensity, you might want to work off the higher end of that formula. In reality, though, you probably will only have room for four 40-watt fluorescent bulbs. In fact, the chart that follows compares the number of bulbs in a typical fluorescent full-hood with the number recommended to keep plants properly. You'll see that the standard equipment often doesn't measure up.

Typical Lighting vs. What Plants Really Need

Tank Size (gallons)	L × W × H (inches)	Typical Full-Hood (# bulbs × watts)
Standard Rectangular Tanks		
2.5	12 × 6 × 8	N/A
5.5	16 × 8 × 10	1 × 8w
10	20 × 10 × 12	1 × 14w
15	24 × 12 × 12	1 × 15w
20XH	20 × 10 × 24	1 × 14w
20H	24 × 12 × 16	1 × 15w
20L	30 × 12 × 12	1 × 20w
29	30 × 12 × 18	1 × 20w
30	36 × 13 × 16	1 × 30w
40	48 × 13 × 16	1 × 40w
44	22 × 22 × 24	2 × 15w
45	36 × 12 × 24	1 × 30w
55	48 × 13 × 20	1 × 40w
*Hexagons**		
10	14 × 12 × 18	1 × 8w
14	14 × 14 × 20	1 × 8w
20	18 × 16 × 20	1 × 14w
27	18 × 18 × 24	1 × 15w
35	23 × 20 × 24	1 × 15w
45	22 × 22 × 24	1 × 15w
60	22 × 22 × 30	1 × 15w
*Flat-Back Hexagons**		
18	24 × 12 × 16	1 × 15w
23	24 × 12 × 20	1 × 15w
26	36 × 12 × 16	1 × 30w
33	36 × 13 × 20	1 × 30w
52	48 × 13 × 20	1 × 40w

*L = diameter measured corner to corner; W = diameter measured pane to pane.

Minimum Lighting for Lush Growth	
Standard Fluorescents (# bulbs × watts)	**Compact Fluorescents** (# bulbs × watts)
1 × 8w	1 × 9w
2 × 8w	2 × 9w
2 × 14w	1 × 28w
2 × 15w	1 × 28w
4 × 15w	2 × 28w
2 × 20w	1 × 55w
2 × 20w	1 × 55w
3 × 20w	1 × 55w
2 × 30w	1 × 55w
2 × 40w	3 × 28w
6 × 15w	4 × 28w
3 × 30w	2 × 55w
3 × 40w	2 × 55w
2 × 8w	2 × 9w
3 × 8w	3 × 9w
3 × 14w	2 × 28w
3 × 15w	2 × 28w
3 × 15w	2 × 28w
4 × 15w	3 × 28w
6 × 15w	4 × 28w
2 × 20w	1 × 55w
2 × 20w	1 × 55w
2 × 30w	1 × 55w
2 × 30w	1 × 55w
3 × 40w	2 × 55w

Fish and Tips

Fluorescent bulbs lose intensity as they age. While the bulb
itself may continue to glow for three years, it will have lost
half its intensity within the first six to 12 months. So
change your bulbs at least once a year. Changing them on
a rotating basis, rather than all at once, is best.

Fertilizers: Step Carefully

Plants need food. They draw nutrients from the water
through their leaves. They draw nutrients from the substrate through their roots. If there is sufficient light and
nutrients, the plants will grow.

As plants grow, they change the conditions in your tank.
Sometimes the change is for the better. For example,
plants can use the carbon dioxide that fish excrete. They
also absorb phosphates and nitrates. So in some ways,
they improve the water quality. However, with the presence of luxuriant plant growth, your tank may become
depleted of necessary nutrients and trace elements. These
nutrients need to be replenished to keep the plants
prospering.

There are two basic things you can do to replenish these
depleted nutrients. The first is to keep up with your regular partial water changes. Partial water changes remove
waste-laden water and replace it with clean water. In the
process, some needed trace elements will be replenished.
The other thing you can do to replace or supplement
these nutrients is to add aquatic plant fertilizers.

Do You Need to Fertilize?

Before I talk about fertilizers, you must first realize that
you may not need them at all. It all depends on your local
conditions. Your local tap water may be full of nitrates,
phosphates, iron, and who knows what. You may find
that your plants grow like crazy without adding fertilizers
and that regular partial water changes are all you need.
Fish excrete waste, which provides nutrients, so the fish
bioload in your aquarium also will be a factor.

If you have only a very few plants, it is probably wise not to
fertilize the tank. Over-fertilization can poison a tank directly, or it could just turn your aquarium into a big algae
farm. Algae are plants, too. So, if the nutrients are there,
and you don't have enough other plants to use them, the
algae will happily feast away on what is available.

Use the condition of your plants to judge the need for
fertilizer. If the light is strong but the growth is slow, you
may need more fertilizer. If the leaves develop yellow
spots or die back, nutrients may be lacking.

What's Available?

Let's look at some common types of fertilizer that you will
find at the local shop.

➤ *Laterite.* This is an iron-rich clay. It comes in several
  forms, including crumbled soil, molded sticks, balls,
  or tablets. Laterite is usually a one-time treatment.
  The crumbled soil is mixed into the lower layer of
  gravel when you first set up the tank, to provide
  iron and nutrients to the plant roots. However, the
  balls, molded sticks, and tablets may be used any
  time as a supplement.

➤ *Granulated.* There is at least one brand of fertilizer
  that looks much like natural aquarium gravel. You
  mix it in the gravel, and it is a slow release fertilizer
  for roots.

➤ *Tablets.* Break these into smaller bits and push them into the gravel near the plant roots. Typically, tablets are used when you make your water changes.

➤ *Liquid.* These mixes are especially good for plants that draw nutrients through their leaves. Liquid fertilizers are usually dosed when you make water changes. Most brands are low in phosphates and nitrates to help prevent algae problems. Liquid iron supplements are especially recommended.

➤ *Carbon dioxide.* Adding CO_2 can be beneficial to all plants. If you add carbon dioxide, you may even find yourself having luck with previously difficult species. The most common way of administering CO_2 is to purchase a kit that contains a small, refillable pressurized cylinder and some type of device for delivering the carbon dioxide to the tank. The output may feed into the input of a canister filter, or it may feed into an inverted plastic bell that goes inside the aquarium.

Starting from the Bottom Up

The first thing I do for my planted tank is to purchase the proper amount of laterite for the particular size aquarium. The packages will tell you what size tank they treat. I mix the laterite with clean aquarium gravel to make a one-inch deep layer on the bottom of the tank.

Next, I add more gravel. Elsewhere in the book, I have recommended keeping a 1.5- to 2-inch-deep layer of gravel. For planted tanks, though, it is best to put in more. You want lots of room for plant roots to grow. You also want to have enough gravel on top of the layer with the laterite to keep it from getting into the water and turning things muddy. So I recommend adding more gravel until you have at least three inches total depth. For bigger tanks, I go four to five inches. (That works out to 20 to 25 pounds of gravel per square foot of bottom.)

Most books on planted aquaria recommend against the use of undergravel filters. Some will go so far as to say that you cannot properly grow plants in a tank that has undergravel filtration. Baloney! I've done it, as have many others. However, I agree that there are disadvantages to having an undergravel filter in a heavily planted tank, though I normally hold them in high regard.

Something's Fishy

Do not use laterite fertilizers with undergravel filter systems. The filter can pull the fertilizer through the gravel bed and kick it back into the tank, clouding the water.

My favorite choice is to use a canister filter. One reason I like them is that most of the components are outside the tank, so they are unobtrusive. Mainly, though, I like canister filters because they are more versatile when it comes to directing the output. Most brands give you the option either of having a single large jet of water return to the tank or of using a perforated spray bar to create several jets.

I prefer to use the spray bar, but instead of mounting it at the back of the tank, like most people do, I mount it at the front. I mount it high enough so that the top frame hides it. If necessary, I purchase additional spray bars and connect them together so that they stretch the entire length of the front of the tank. Then I twist the various sections of spray bar to point them where I need current. Some will spray across the surface for circulation and aeration. Some will point more toward the bottom to keep the debris blowing toward the filter intake.

An added benefit of this method is that, by directing the current from front to back instead of back to front, it helps keep the plants standing up straight. Assuming you planted your large plants in the rear of the tank, when the current is piped from behind, it blows the plants over. The taller ones shade the lower ones, starving them of light. By piping water from the front toward the back, it helps keep the tall plants pushed back a bit, so that the lower plants and the plants in front can get light, too. It also keeps heavy plant growth from completely overgrowing the surface and choking out the influx of fresh oxygen.

Dig Those Crazy Plants

You probably have an idea of what you want your tank to look like. But even if you are wading right in without a preplanned decoration scheme, this part is fun. The placement of the plants will be up to you. You are going to paint your own three-dimensional landscape masterpiece.

Try to make your setup look natural. Group species of plants together, don't make a symmetrical display, don't plant in rows, and (in most cases) put taller plants to the back. Perhaps you have a plant that would make a good centerpiece, although you don't want to plant it exactly in the center of the tank. Setting it to one side will look more natural. You can leave one large, open space for the fish to swim, or make several smaller connected spaces. Be creative!

It would be easy for me to tell you to just shove the plants down in the gravel and tamp the gravel around them to hold them down, but it isn't always that simple. Plants grow in different ways, and they root in different ways, too. So let me give you a few pointers on planting plants.

Bunch plants are quite versatile. You can plant each stem singly, or plant the whole bunch as a group, or break the bunch up into two or more smaller groups. Whatever

looks good to you is going to be perfect for your tank.
Most bunch plants eventually will grow roots, but since
what you are buying are clippings off larger plants, the
roots will likely not be there yet. To plant, simply push
about one inch of the stem into the gravel and tamp
gravel around the plant to hold it in place.

Crown plants will often come with extensive root systems.
You may even need to take some scissors and trim the
roots down to an inch or two in length. The easiest way to
plant these is to first plant them a little deeper than ideal,
then tug gently until the base (crown) of the plant is
above the gravel line. Then tamp down the gravel around
the plant to firmly hold the roots in place.

With floating plants, there is nothing to plant. Just toss
them in the tank, and they float around. Your main concern is to be sure the plant is right side up, if it has a top
and bottom. Watersprite, for example, has a top and bottom (roots dangle from the bottom), while riccia, wolffia,
and hornwort do not produce roots. They tumble with the
current.

Don't go overboard on the floating plants. Since they
grow right at the surface, they block much of the light
that would otherwise shine on the plants down below.
If your floating plants get overgrown, don't be afraid to
harvest some from the tank so that the other plants can
prosper, too.

Fit and Trimmed

Once your tank becomes established, you will need to do
some occasional trimming and replanting. Pruning plants
gets rid of dead leaves, reshapes a plant to fit its environment, removes extra growth that is blocking the light, and
removes growth that is sparse or spindly.

When bunch plants get too long, you can prune them by pinching off the tops. In fact, you can improve the appearance of many species in this manner, because two stems will grow from the pinch point. So the plant should get bushier with the proper trimming. Plus, you can plant the part that you pinched off and it will form a brand new stem.

Sometimes the stems of bunch plants lose their lower leaves. This may be caused by damage, old age, or lack of light in the lower part of the tank. In any case, you may want to trim these plants by digging them out, pinching off the scraggly bottom portion, and then replanting the leafy top.

With crown plants, the only trimming you want to do is to remove dead leaves. Always pinch them off as close to the bottom as possible. If you see a leaf dying on a crown plant, it is better to remove it immediately rather than waiting for the whole leaf to wilt. As long as the leaf is partially alive, it saps strength from the rest of the plant.

It is not uncommon for some species to shed leaves when transplanted—especially some crown plants, and especially if they grew emersed (above the water). Many of the

Chapter 15

Aw, Gee! Is That Algae?

In This Chapter

➤ Learn what algae is

➤ Discover what causes it

➤ Find out how to control it

Algae is something every aquarist has to deal with. If nothing else, it will occasionally need to be wiped from the glass to give you the clearest view of your fish. And for some hobbyists, algae will grow in epidemic proportions and be a continuous battle. In this chapter I'll explain what algae is, if it's harmful, how to prevent it from getting out of hand, and what to do if it does.

What's It All About, Algae?

When aquarists think of algae, they usually think of it as a pest. It can be, but it really isn't. Algae exists in every aquatic system, and even if you start out with a sterile tank, spores in the air will introduce algae to the system. Algae is everywhere, and is a natural, normal part of an ecosystem.

Now, it is true that algae can take over a tank and be a problem. Still, rather than think of algae as a pest, it's better to think of it as a signpost. It can tell you a lot about the condition of your tank. Use algae as an indicator. Algae will not grow out of balance unless there is something out of balance in the system.

Fish School

Algae (pronounced *AL-jee*) is plural for alga (pronounced *AL-guh*). Alga may be used to refer to a single algal (pronounced *AL-gul*) organism, or to a single species. Algae is plural for both. There is no such word as "algaes."

In fact, that overabundance of algae *may* be doing you a favor. Think about it. If your tank is so loaded with nutrients that you are growing bumper crops of algae, what would that tank be like without the algae? The algae are removing those nutrients and storing them, until you remove the algae. If the algae weren't binding up those nutrients, your fish would be swimming in a soup with a stronger organic content. That is not good.

Light Plus Nutrients Equals Algae

Excess algae growth can be blamed on two things: too much light (or too much of the wrong wavelength) and too many nutrients. Controlling one or both factors can create conditions unsuitable for algae growth. Of course, it needs to be done in such a way that you don't starve the other plants and animals in your system of light and nutrients, too.

Light

Algae need light to photosynthesize. Without light, they die. Controlling the amount and type of light also may control your algae problem. Review your lighting situation. Based on the chart in Chapter 14, do you have enough light to grow plants well? Can you cut back a bit to inhibit algae? Would running your light for fewer hours per day be beneficial? Are you using the proper full-spectrum bulbs, or did you pick a bulb of the wrong spectrum to save money?

Nutrients

Like all living things, plants need food. They take in nutrients through their roots and through their leaves. If your system has nutrient overload, algae is going to get a foothold. Is the tank overcrowded? Excess fish waste adds nutrients to the tank. Are you over fertilizing or fertilizing when it isn't necessary?

Shortages of nutrients may cause algae, too. You see, if there are nutrients in the water, some plant form will use them. If they are in the proper balance to grow desirable aquatic plants, those plants should prosper and outcompete the algae. However, if the nutrients are insufficient for higher plant forms or if they are in the wrong proportions, conditions may be created that are more beneficial for the algae, and so the algae may get the upper hand.

Are you keeping up with your scheduled maintenance, particularly your partial water changes? Partial water changes remove dissolved waste and replace depleted trace elements. Even if your aquatic plants are growing well and algae isn't present, those plants are removing nutrients from the water and, therefore, changing the quality of that water. Without regular partial water changes to stabilize things, water quality will deteriorate and may create conditions that are more suitable for algae growth.

Fish and Tips

Using sodium biphosphate to reduce pH may contribute to algae problems. Algae can use phosphates as food.

Run some water tests. If your tank suddenly has an algae problem, are any of the water quality parameters testing at abnormal levels? Checking pH, general hardness, carbonate hardness, nitrate, and phosphate may give you a clue.

Even if you are doing nothing different, a sudden bloom of algae may be linked to changes in your local tap water. Seasonal variances, including heavy rains, can affect the chemistry of your local water. Using test kits to regularly monitor your water quality can help you troubleshoot your tank.

Herbivores You'll Adore

The easiest way to control algae is to get some live-in janitors. All you have to do is buy a few algae-eating critters. Not only will they help control algae problems, but you'll have fun watching them do it.

Algae-eating fish are the first, best defense. There are several species of fish that eat algae. The ones I most recommend are the various varieties of plecostomus (suckermouth cats) and otocinclus (the pygmy sucker cats).

Shrimp are good at reaching places that the algae-eating fish can't reach. There are several species of shrimp that are sold for aquariums. All will nibble at algae to one extent or the other. Ghost shrimp and Malaysian rainbow shrimp are good ones for nibbling at beard and brush algae.

All snails will eat some algae. Some are better than others, though. Avoid apple snails and Colombian ramshorn snails if you have live plants. They want to eat the plants, too. Even the smaller species of ramshorn and pond snails are sometimes to blame for munching softer plants. If you add snails to your tank, do it because you want to watch them. Don't expect them to be all that great at eating algae.

If your snails over-multiply, consider buying a clown loach. This peaceful, attractive fish loves to eat them. *Do not* buy the snail-killing potions! They may kill your plants. Plus, all those dead snails will pollute the tank and kill fish. You also can squash the occasional snail against the aquarium glass, and the fish will all nibble at the meat.

Die, Algae! Die!

Unfortunately, the natural method of algae control doesn't always work, or isn't always enough. You may have lots of live plants to compete with the algae, and a good complement of grazers to nibble at it, but all this still may not be enough. In that case, you are going to have to pitch in and deal with some algae yourself.

Even in the best situation, you will occasionally need to wipe algae from your glass. I highly recommend the algae scrubber pads sold in pet stores. Buy the ones without the handles, as they are much easier to use on the hard-to-reach spots. The scrubber pad can be used on the glass, and on some rocks and decorations. For really tough algae on the glass, a razor blade type of scraper works well.

There are several sizes and styles of bottle brushes designed for cleaning algae from filter tubes. There are rigid versions for straight tubes and flexible versions for getting into the bends of siphon and intake tubes. If necessary, you also can remove ornaments from your tank and take them to the sink to scrub with any soap-free household brush.

Something's Fishy

Never use household sponges or scrubbing pads to clean inside your tank. They may contain soap or chemicals. This applies even to brand-new ones. For example, put a brand-new cellulose sponge in a sink of water and squeeze it a few times. Look at all the suds!

Bleach can be another option. I hesitate to recommend this because you can easily kill your fish. However, non-living decorations can be *removed from the tank,* scrubbed, and then given a short soak in a solution of bleach—say, one cup of bleach per gallon of water. Afterwards, be sure to rinse the decorations well. Even better, soak them in a bucket with some extra dechlorinator to neutralize any bleach that you missed before returning the items to the tank. *Never put bleach into your tank* or use it to clean live plants. Use bleach at your own risk!

There are several products on the market that are specifically designed to kill algae in the tank. Used as directed, they are *normally* safe to put in with the fish. However, I recommend using algicides *only as a last resort,* as they may kill your plants. Use algicides at your own risk!

Other chemicals, called flocculents, can be added to the water where they will cause small particulates to clump into larger particles that can be more easily removed by the filter system. They also help with green water problems that are caused by free-floating algae.

Making It Perfectly Clear

Turbidity (cloudiness) is a problem sometimes encountered in the aquarium. Since one type of algae is a possible cause, I've decided to talk about cloudy water in this chapter.

Green Water

This is the "pea soup" condition caused by unicellular free-floating algae. There are so many of them in suspension that they form a green haze. Green water can be particularly difficult to cure. It may appear suddenly, with no obvious cause, and it may disappear just as quickly.

To treat green water, try reducing light or reducing nutrients first. Try adding live plants. If those methods don't work, then try one of the flocculating products. If that fails, an algicide may be necessary.

Or, you could just be patient. Eventually, green water will clear on its own. It uses up nutrients and dies back, or microscopic organisms that eat it will eventually clear it away.

Milky Water

Bacterial bloom is one cause of cloudy water. It is more common in new tanks, and many refer to it as "new tank syndrome." An established aquarium has a healthy balance of bacteria and microorganisms. A new tank does not. With the right combination of nutrients in the water, some types of bacteria may supermultiply as they feed on the nutrients. There may be so many bacteria that they will cloud the tank.

This problem will usually fix itself in a couple of days, or it may take a week or so. The bacteria deplete the nutrients and die off. So the best way to deal with bacterial bloom is to wait it out. Of course, be sure that you aren't contributing to it by overfeeding.

Suspended particulates are another cause of cloudy water. Usually, the particulates will be single-celled algae or the bacteria that have bloomed, as I just described. However, the particulates may be microscopic debris. For example, they could be dust from new aquarium gravel that wasn't properly rinsed before it was introduced into the tank. You may want to try flocculents to combat this problem.

Chapter 16

Stress and Disease

In This Chapter

➤ How stress affects your fish

➤ Danger signals you should watch for

➤ Common diseases of aquarium fish

➤ Typical treatments and preferred medications

➤ Quarantining new arrivals

➤ Euthanizing terminal cases

What is it that causes disease and death in your fish? Your first instinct may be to say germs. Sometimes that is true, but usually when disease organisms get a foothold in your fish tank it is not so much that they are a cause—more likely, they are an effect. You probably noticed that I titled this chapter "Stress and Disease." Notice that I mentioned stress before I mentioned disease.

Don't Stress Me Out!

Stress is the major cause of disease and death in fish. How do I define stress? Basically, it's anything that makes your fish unhappy. When your fish are under stress, they will be more susceptible to disease. Pathogens are everywhere. There is no avoiding them. However, happy, healthy fish are normally able to fight them off quite easily. Their immune systems do their jobs well, and the fish stay healthy. Stressed-out fish have compromised immune systems.

What are some things that can cause stress in a fish? It shouldn't be surprising that the things that stress your fish are the same things that stress you and me. Let's look at the common stressors, one by one.

➤ *Hunger.* A fish that is getting insufficient nutrition is a fish with lowered immunity. A starving fish is also more likely to try to take a nip out of someone else, or to be attacked by the others in the aquarium.

➤ *Overcrowding.* This will cause territories to overlap more, resulting in more fights. It also will cause the tank to have higher waste levels, which can poison a fish directly, create breeding grounds for pathogens, affect appetite, and compromise immunity.

➤ *Rapid temperature changes.* Fish are more likely to get sick when subjected to extremes in temperature. A proper aquarium heater helps prevent dramatic temperature changes. When making water changes, you also need to match the temperature of the new water to that of the old water.

➤ *Lack of rest.* Fish don't sleep quite the way we do, but they do go into a resting state. It is important that they get the chance. Be sure to turn out the lights on your tank at night.

➤ *Loud noises.* It is probably not a good idea to put your stereo speakers next to an aquarium. Also, don't play that music so loud! Your fish will appreciate it, and so will your neighbors. Setting the aquarium on top of the television is probably a bad idea, as well.

➤ *Bullies.* Constant nips not only do physical damage, they keep a fish from getting adequate nutrition and rest. Further, wounds make easy entry points for infections. Mixing compatible species will help prevent this problem.

What's Wrong with That Fishy in the Window?

Fish are fairly good at giving warning signs of impending doom. You just need to know what to watch for. Following are some danger signals:

➤ *Listlessness.* When a fish that is normally active suddenly starts lying around or hiding, it's a sign that something is amiss. Causes of listlessness include deteriorated water quality, parasites, overeating, injury, and incorrect water temperatures. Be aware that some territorial species may be quite active in your tank when first introduced, but once they settle in they will pick a spot and stay there. That is normal. Also, livebearers about to give birth may take to hiding or resting in preparation. Again, that would be normal behavior.

➤ *Loss of appetite.* If your fish stops eating, unless you have just stuffed him with a heavy meal, it's a bad sign. Most fish are hungry practically all of the time. Poor water quality, bullies, disease, and spoiled food are possible causes of loss of appetite.

➤ *Color changes*. Many things can cause a fish to change color. Some of them are good. Some are bad. Fish will change color to blend into the background. It's Mother Nature's way of camouflaging the fish from predators. Also, a fish that is about to breed is usually going to take on darker, brighter colors. This is good! The fish is happy.

Watch, though, for color changes that seem abnormal or have no apparent reasonable cause. If a fish's color suddenly fades, it is probably under some type of stress—although, if it fades over time, it may be diet related. If discolored patches develop, the fish may be coming down with a disease.

Some species will change pattern drastically, say from blotched to striped, when excited. Also, most fish will fade at night. Anyway, be sure you are familiar with what is normal for the species you keep.

➤ *Clamped fins*. The fins of most species will be spread and erect when healthy. If these fish suddenly start keeping their fins folded against the body, it is a danger signal. Other fish, like the popular algae-eating plecostomus, will normally keep their fins folded, erecting them only when swimming or when excited.

➤ *Shimmies*. Sometimes clamped fins are accompanied by shimmying. This symptom is best described as the fish swimming in one place, wagging its body from side to side. Mostly, we see this problem with livebearing fish, but gouramies or others may get it, too. Common causes are low temperature or incorrect water chemistry.

➤ *Distended gills*. A fish that is holding its gills open is a fish that is having major troubles. Many things can cause this, including gill parasites, toxins in the water, and gill damage. High ammonia levels or low pH levels are major causes.

➤ *Rapid breathing or gasping at the surface.* Both are signs that a fish is not getting sufficient oxygen. Possible causes are low levels of dissolved oxygen in the tank, high waste levels that prevent proper exchange of oxygen, gill damage from parasites, or the presence of toxins in the water.

➤ *Split or frayed fins.* Split fins are usually a result of a fight. In most cases, do nothing. The fins will heal nicely without help. However, if the edges of the fins become ragged or show signs of decay, it could be a sign of disease or even poor water quality.

➤ *Sores and wounds.* Again, aggression is usually the cause, but advanced infections also can open sores on your fish.

➤ *Cloudy eyes.* There are some diseases that cause this problem, but it is more likely to be due to insufficient water changes resulting in low pH or high ammonia. Occasionally, the problem may be cataracts.

➤ *Swollen stomach.* A swollen stomach may indicate gluttony, a female fish full of roe, internal parasites, or it could mean that your fish has fluid buildup from the disease, dropsy.

➤ *Emaciated stomach.* If a fish is losing weight, be sure you are offering the proper diet. Poor water quality can affect appetite, and parasites are a likely cause of skinny fish.

➤ *Bent spine.* A fish with a bent spine was probably born that way, and will likely be fine. However, a fish that develops a bent spine later in life is probably suffering from a diet deficiency or an injury.

➤ *White slimy patches.* Your fish excretes extra slime as a defense against infection. The problem is a little hard to diagnose without a microscope because protozoa, bacteria, flukes, and just plain lousy water quality can all cause a fish to slime up.

➤ *Erratic or unusual behavior.* Get to know what is normal for the species you keep, and you will catch problems much earlier. For example, a bottom feeder that suddenly spends all of its time hanging around at the surface is exhibiting unusual behavior.

Make It a Habit to Check the Habitat

If you spot any of the warning signs I just listed, what do you do first? That's right, curse aloud—unless there are kids nearby. Next, visually check the environment. Remember that stress is the most common cause of problems, so here are some questions to ask yourself:

➤ Has an air line become disconnected?

➤ Is a filter clogged?

➤ When was the last water change?

➤ What is the current water temperature?

➤ Is there a bully in the tank?

➤ Is the tank too dirty?

➤ Are there obvious symptoms of infection?

You're not done checking the environment, yet. Even if there are no obvious equipment problems or any signs of disease, you should run your water tests for pH, ammonia, and nitrite. You cannot measure water quality by looking at it with the naked eye. Test the water!

Obviously, if your water tests show that the water quality is out of whack, you will need to take corrective action. See Chapters 10 and 11 on cycling a new tank and water quality for help with that. Sometimes a partial water change is all your fish need to correct a problem.

Also obvious, if there are visible signs of infection, you will need to medicate your fish. Let me tell you about some common diseases. Afterward, I'll discuss various treatments.

Dots, Spots, Patches, and Fuzz

Most diseases of aquarium fish will show up as dots, spots, patches, or fuzz somewhere on the outside of the fish. Some diseases are quite easy to identify by sight. Others will require some educated guesswork, unless you have access to a decent microscope.

Ick! My Fish Has Ich

There are many nasty protozoans that attack fish. Some of them are true parasites, but some are merely opportunistic organisms taking advantage of already sick or dying fish.

Probably the most well-known protozoan parasite of fish is ich. Ich is so well-known that many new hobbyists seem to want to diagnose every disease as ich. Ich is pronounced *ick* and is short for the name of the offending organism, *Ichthyophthirius multifilius*. Most hobbyists see this parasite at one time or another, so let's talk about how to characterize the symptoms of ich.

Imagine, if you will, that you are holding your fish in one hand and a salt shaker in the other. Now, imagine that you sprinkle some salt on the fish. You have just visualized the exact appearance of a fish infected with ich—except, of course, that you won't be holding a slimy fish in your hand. Ick!

Ich appears as a spattering of tiny white dots the size of salt crystals. It may first present itself as a dot or two on the fins or body, and later spread. If left untreated long enough, the fish will begin to look more slimy than dotted. This is due to massive tissue damage—the fish will then produce extra body slime, seeking some relief. If your fish gets to this state, the odds of saving it will be much lower. Too much damage will have been done.

This marble hatchetfish has an ich infection.

However, you are not going to let your fish get to that state, are you? Ich is quite easy to spot, and if you catch it early and provide proper treatment, you shouldn't lose a single fish to it. Ever! I wish all fish diseases were as easy to treat as ich.

Treating Ich

There are many effective drugs available, but you need to keep something in mind. These drugs don't kill the parasite when it is attached to the fish or when it is in the encysted reproduction stage on the bottom of the tank. The medication only works on the free-swimming stages of the parasite. Therefore, it is important that you don't stop treating the fish when the last dot disappears. Treat for at least one more day to be sure you get all the trophonts.

You will find many brands of ich medication on the market. Some are more effective than others, and some are safer than others. Most will contain various combinations of formalin (dilute formaldehyde), malachite green (a dye), or a solution of copper.

My favorite is a straight malachite green formulation. I've been using it for over 30 years. It works. It's relatively safe, and it's usually the cheapest choice. It will turn your water slightly blue at first, but the color will fade away within a few hours. Note, though, that some tetras and scaleless bottom fish can be sensitive to this medication, and it should only be used at half dosage with those fish. Follow the manufacturer's instructions for dosage of the brand you choose.

Formalin-malachite green formulations are also quite popular. I sometimes use this combination to treat other, more difficult protozoal infestations. In combination, formalin and malachite green have a synergistic effect, meaning the two ingredients are safer and stronger together than when used alone.

If this is so, why don't I use this combination for ich, too? It's because I find that ich is plenty easy to treat, and that using malachite green alone requires no extra water changes during treatment. Formalin, on the other hand, does more harm to the biological filtration in the tank, may cloud the water, and stinks. After treating with a product that contains formalin, you will need to change some water to get your water quality back in order.

There are some copper formulations available for treating ich, but I don't much like them. Their efficacy depends on such factors as whether they are chelated (pronounced *KEY-lay-ted*) and the hardness of your water. Copper medications are dangerous if you have soft water. Copper is hard on plants, too. In other words, they may work, but they also may be dangerous or useless.

Bacterial Infections

Bacteria are much smaller than protozoa, but they tend to grow in colonies, so resulting infections may be more easily visible to your eye than protozoal infections. Typically, bacterial infections will show as slimy patches developing on the skin of the fish. Sometimes they will be bloody. Fin rot (as opposed to split or damaged fins) and mouth rot (often erroneously called mouth fungus) will probably be due to bacterial infections.

Antibiotics will be necessary to treat bacterial infections. It is important that you treat quickly, too, as these infections can spread extremely quickly. Some will kill your fish within hours of the symptoms first appearing!

Your pet store probably will carry a variety of antibiotics. Some are effective. Some are not. In a moment, I will steer you toward the better ones, but you must remember that the best you can do is take an educated *guess* about which is the right choice. Why? Because no antibiotic treats every bacterial infection. They all will be effective against some bacteria, but not against others.

In fact, many antibiotics don't kill bacteria in the first place! Instead, they mess up the reproductive ability of the bacteria, so that the bacteria stop multiplying. This lets the immune system of the host catch up and do the job of eliminating the infection.

Fish and Tips

Some antibiotics come as tablets, some as gel-caps. The tablets can usually be dropped directly into the aquarium without crushing. The gel-caps should be opened, and the powder inside should be poured into the aquarium. Dispose of the empty capsules.

A Cure for What Ails

Since there are many brands of anitbiotics out there and I have no way of knowing which ones your local shops carry, I'll give you the names of the active ingredients. I recommend you avoid choosing medications that don't list the active ingredients. For one thing, you won't know what you are getting. For another, if that medication doesn't work, how do you know that the next thing you try isn't the same medicine under a different brand name?

Here are some of my favorite antibiotics:

➤ Kanamycin sulphate

➤ Furan drugs

➤ Sulfa drugs

➤ Chloramphenicol

➤ Minocyline

➤ Neomycin sulphate

Fish and Tips

If you choose tetracycline as a treatment, you may want to use the oral form. You can purchase "medicated flake" fish food that contains this drug. The advantage of oral medication is that it puts the drug inside the fish, where it will do the most good. Of course, your fish must be eating for it to work.

A Fungus Among Us

True fungus, caused by the organism *Saprolegnia,* is quite distinctive from the various bacterial infections that are often mislabeled as fungus ("mouth fungus"). True fungus is fuzzy. In advanced stages, it is even hairy looking. It looks a bit like a dandelion head that has gone to seed. Assuming your eyesight is decent, you will be able to see actual filaments. True fungus is the fuzzy stuff that you see growing on dead, rotting fish, or perhaps on uneaten fish food that is lying about the tank.

True fungus is a secondary infection. The spores that produce it are everywhere, but a healthy, undamaged fish will never catch it. True fungus infects dead tissue. So if you have a fish that has dead tissue from an injury, it may contract fungus. If your fish has an advanced protozoal or bacterial infection that has caused tissue to die, fungus may set in as well.

This disease is difficult to treat, probably because you can't cure dead tissue. It sets roots deep into the flesh of the fish, which may make the situation worse by killing more tissue. There are some medications that may help. They can retard the growth of the fungus. These include sodium chlorite solutions, methylene blue, and potassium permanganate. Formalin and malachite green combinations may have some effect, as well.

One treatment involves netting the fish and dabbing some mercurochrome or Betadine directly onto the infected area. In severe cases, I find it helps to take some tweezers and try to pull off as much of the fungus as possible before applying the treatment.

False Fungus

You may also run across a protozoan masquerading as a fungus. It's the *Epistylis,* a protozoan shaped like the stem and flower of a tulip. It usually grows in colonies. Sometimes, it can be found infecting fish—particularly growing as a tuft on the edge, or at the base of the fins. Unfortunately, a colony of epistylis can become large enough that it looks fuzzy like a colony of fungus. In fact, fungus may be growing right along with the protozoan. Anyway, formalin–malachite green will clear up epistylis in a few days. So if your fungus medication doesn't seem to be working, you may want to treat with formalin–malachite green or another antiprotozoal remedy.

The Worms Go In, the Worms Go Out

Worms are not just good food for fish. Sometimes, fish are good food for worms! Of course, we're not talking about the same type of worms that you would feed your fish. There are many worm species that are internal or external parasites of fish.

It should come as no surprise that fish, like many other animals, can get tapeworms and other intestinal worms. Unfortunately, it is difficult to diagnose these problems without sacrificing a fish and examining the contents of its guts under the microscope. If your fish has internal worms, the odds are that they are present in low numbers. Generally, no action is needed. A healthy fish can live just fine with an occasional parasite. In severe infections, you can try to medicate.

You probably will have a hard time finding worm medication for your fish. There just aren't many commercial preparations available for fish, without going through a veterinarian. Treating internal worms isn't easy. Picking the right medication and delivering it where it can work is difficult. Butyl tin oxide, praziquantel, piperazine, levamisole, mebendazole, flubendazole, and mebendazole are common ingredients.

Just a Fluke

The flukes are an interesting group of worms. Many have an encysted larval form that is just plain untreatable. If the numbers present are low, it's no big deal. If the fish is heavily infested, its chances are not so good.

Most of the types of worm that infect fish infest them from the inside. However, some types live on the skin and gills. Skin and gill flukes are sort of like microscopic leeches. They have grasping hooks at one end and a mouth at the other. They move about your fish in inch-worm fashion.

It will take a microscope to make a definite diagnosis, but if your fish scratches on rocks, or if the gills have become distended, it may be infested with flukes. Also, bloody patches may result from a heavy infestation. Fortunately, skin and gill flukes are easy to treat. There are several medications on the market. Praziquantel, various organo-phosphates, fenbendazol, flubendazole, mebendazole, potassium permanganate, or copper can be used. Check with your dealer.

Professionals often use Dylox, an herbicide, for treating external flukes. If you find a medication that lists trichlorofon or dimethyl trichloro hydroxethyl phosphonate (with some numbers mixed in the formula), it is probably a good bet. But be careful! This stuff is carcinogenic.

Other Assorted Maladies

Fish can also get sick in other ways. I'll look at some of the most common problems and how to treat them.

Swimbladder Problems

This manifests itself as a buoyancy problem, with the fish swimming loop-de-loops, or floating upside down, or having trouble rising from the bottom of the tank.

The swimbladder is a gas-filled balloon inside most species of fish. It lets the fish maintain the proper buoyancy in the water, and it helps keep the fish in an upright position. However, the swimbladder sometimes fails. There are many possible causes for this, including infection, injury, genetic defects, rapid temperature changes, and so forth. The condition is normally not contagious, but is rarely treatable.

Popeye

Sometimes things go wrong, and it's enough to make your fish's eyes bug out! Popeye is a condition where gas or fluid builds up behind the eye, popping it from its socket. Sometimes an antibiotic will help this condition. Sometimes it goes away on its own.

Dropsy

This condition is not so much a disease as it is a symptom. The fish swells with fluids, and if you look at it from above, you will see the scales standing out on edge giving a pine cone appearance. The tank water may be too hard, or the fish may have an infection. Raising the salt level to two or three teaspoons per gallon may help, along with the addition of a good antibiotic.

Hole in the Head

The common name for this disease, more correctly called head and lateral line erosion (or HLLE), describes a typical symptom. Fish have sensory pores on their faces, and running down their sides is a row of tiny pores that form the lateral line. Sometimes, these pores become irritated and develop into pale open pits. There may be a bit of exudate (that's stuff oozing out—aren't you sorry you asked?).

Over the years, many things have been blamed for causing HLLE. Some early hobbyists saw strands of exudate coming from the sores, leading them to blame the problem on worms. Others claimed that the protozoan *Hexamita* was the cause. Still others have blamed diet, induced voltage from aquarium pumps, viruses, and so on. The truth is that no one really knows. Except the worm theory, there is probably some truth to all of the other possibilities.

However, I will tell you this. In over 30 years, I have never seen a freshwater fish develop HLLE when kept in stores with central filter systems. In fact, I've seen many fish cured of the problem, with no additional treatment, when put into these systems. Also, the only freshwater fish that seem to get HLLE are large fish in crowded conditions.

I firmly believe that water quality is the biggest single cause of HLLE. So if you have a fish that develops this problem, change more water, more often. If you aren't varying the diet, do so. Better nutrition is always good. You may want to treat with metronidazole, in case there is a secondary Hexamita infection.

Viral Infection

Fish also get viruses, but we know little about them and there are no treatments available anyway. So, this will be a short topic! The only viral infection that you may be able to identify is *lymphocystis*. This disease is not very common, but it does show up on certain species with some regularity. The virus causes cartilaginous tissue to rapidly multiply, forming little nodules. Usually, the nodules form on the rays of the fins, but sometimes on the body, too. They start out looking like ich. That is, you will see isolated single dots first. As the disease progresses, the dots develop into cauliflower-like growths.

The bad news is that there is no treatment for lymphocystis. However, extra water changes may help. The problem is more common on salt-loving species, so be sure you have met their needs in that regard. Sometimes, you can take a razor blade, scrape off the nodules *(very carefully!),* dab the wound with mercurochrome, and the problem may not return.

The good news is that lymphocystis will usually spontaneously remit in a few weeks. So your fish should eventually cure itself. Technically, the disease is considered contagious. In my experience, though, that is rarely the case.

Anyway, there are many other diseases that your fish can get. If you'd like to learn more, I recommend you check your pet shop for *The Manual of Fish Health* by Dr. Chris Andrews, published by Tetra Press. The book has great photos of sick fish, making it easier for you to identify diseases.

This Is Your Fish on Drugs

You probably will find that your aquarium store has a large selection of fish medications. It will be quite confusing to choose, because every brand and medication is going to make great claims about itself. There are even some brands that make absolutely false claims about what they can do. The fish medication industry isn't as highly regulated as the human medication industry. On one hand, this is bad, because there is less rigorous testing, less quality control, and more exaggerated claims. On the other hand, many of these medications are the same ones given to humans, but are sold at a fraction of the cost that your pharmacist would charge.

I have talked about symptoms, diseases, and possible medications to use. Now, I want to give you some guidelines for using those medications.

> ➤ Before medicating, check the environment. Be sure the filters are working properly and the temperature is correct, and also run some water tests for pH, ammonia, and nitrite.

➤ If it has been more than a week since your last partial water change, change some now. Water changes are very important. Medications degrade water quality. I recommend that you change some water every day during any drug treatment, but minimally I recommend a partial water change before, halfway through, and after treatment is complete.

➤ Remove activated carbon from the filters. Activated carbon removes many medications from the water!

➤ Follow the manufacturer's directions to achieve a therapeutic dose of the medication. Too little of a drug will render it ineffective. Too much can be toxic to your fish.

➤ Evaluate the treatment. Watch your fish for changes. I recommend that you treat three days before you evaluate. Then, do the following:

— If the fish is cured, treatment can be discontinued, although it is better to continue for a full five to seven days, to play it safe.

— If the fish has improved but is not cured, continue the treatment a bit longer.

— If the fish is the same or worse, the treatment is not working. Change some water and try a different drug.

Quarantine and Hospitalization

I am about to give you a good piece of advice—advice that you probably will ignore. If you do, don't say I never told you so. Before introducing new fish to your tank (except the very first batch, of course) I recommend that you quarantine them for two weeks in a separate tank. This greatly lessens the chance that you'll introduce a disease to your aquarium.

A quarantine tank can be quite simple. It can be a five- or 10-gallon bare aquarium with an el-cheapo filter in it (I prefer sponge filters for this application) and a rock or plant to provide cover for the fish. When you're not using the tank for quarantine, it can be used as a hospital tank to treat a sick fish or let an injured one recover. It also makes a good tank for raising baby fish, when not otherwise in use. You probably can put together a quarantine tank for under $20.

Fish and Tips

Consider sterilizing your nets after each use and between aquariums. Nets can transfer disease. There are commercial preparations you can buy to make a sterilizing net soak, or merely mix some bleach and water in a bucket and let the net soak a bit. Rise *thoroughly* to remove all the bleach.

Sample Shopping Lists

My friend Elaine once told me that she wished there had been an aquarium book with some sample shopping lists when she started her first tank. It would have been easier if she could have walked into a store with a list of exactly what she needed.

Now there is such a book! Following are some sample shopping lists for a few popular sizes of aquariums. I made it even easier by including some brand names, where appropriate. I chose quality brands that have wide distribution, so you shouldn't have trouble finding any of the items. Still, these are just guidelines—don't be afraid to let your dealer substitute equivalents.

Each shopping list includes:

➤ A list of equipment

➤ A list of hardy live plants that can survive with only a standard full-hood; add more light if you want to keep more diverse plant species

➤ A first batch of hardy fish to cycle the tank

➤ A second batch to fill out the tank, after it has cycled

10-Gallon Small-Tank Shopping List

Equipment

- ❏ 10-gallon Perfecto or All-Glass aquarium
- ❏ 20-inch full-hood with fluorescent light
- ❏ Aqua-Clear Mini power filter
- ❏ 50-watt heater
- ❏ thermometer
- ❏ 15 pounds of aquarium gravel
- ❏ TetraMin fish food
- ❏ four-inch fish net
- ❏ Stress Coat water conditioner
- ❏ beginner's book
- ❏ rocks, driftwood, decorations of your choice

Fish (Batch 1)

- ❏ 3 zebra or pearl danios
- ❏ 3 platies

Fish (Batch 2)

- ❏ 4 neon tetras
- ❏ 2 corydoras catfish
- ❏ 1 otocinclus

Plants

- ❏ 6 vallisneria
- ❏ 2 bunches anacharis
- ❏ 2 bunches rotala indica
- ❏ 1 amazon swordplant

29-Gallon Medium Tank Shopping List

Equipment

- ❏ 29-gallon Perfecto or All-Glass aquarium
- ❏ 30-inch full-hood with fluorescent light
- ❏ Aqua-Clear 200 power filter
- ❏ 150-watt heater
- ❏ thermometer
- ❏ 30 pounds of aquarium gravel
- ❏ TetraMin fish food
- ❏ 5-inch fish net
- ❏ Stress Coat water conditioner
- ❏ beginner's book
- ❏ rocks, driftwood, decorations of your choice

Fish (Batch 1)

- ❏ 3 silver or marble hatchets
- ❏ 3 platies
- ❏ 6 black tetras
- ❏ 3 corydoras catfish

Fish (Batch 2)

- ❏ 6 neon tetras
- ❏ 6 harlequin rasbora
- ❏ 3 otocinclus *or*
- ❏ 1 small plecostomus

Plants

- ❏ 6 vallisneria
- ❏ 2 bunches anacharis
- ❏ 2 bunches rotala indica
- ❏ 3 bunches hygrophila polysperma
- ❏ 1 Amazon swordplant

55-Gallon Large Tank Shopping List

Equipment

- ❑ 55-gallon Perfecto or All-Glass aquarium
- ❑ 48-inch full-hood with 48-inch fluorescent light
- ❑ Aqua-Clear 300 power filter
- ❑ 60 pounds of aquarium gravel
- ❑ 200-watt heater
- ❑ thermometer
- ❑ TetraMin fish food
- ❑ 6-inch fish net
- ❑ Stress Coat water conditioner
- ❑ beginner's book
- ❑ rocks, driftwood, decorations of your choice

Fish (Batch 1)

- ❑ 6 zebra or pearl danios
- ❑ 6 platies
- ❑ 6 tiger barbs
- ❑ 12 serpae tetras

Fish (Batch 2)

- ❑ 12 large neon tetras
- ❑ 2 kissing gouramies
- ❑ 1 pair kribensis
- ❑ 3 clown loaches
- ❑ 6 corydoras cats
- ❑ 6 otocinclus *or*
- ❑ 3 otocinclus and 1 small plecostomus

Plants

- ❏ 12 vallisneria
- ❏ 2 bunches anacharis
- ❏ 4 bunches rotala indica
- ❏ 4 bunches hygrophila polysperma
- ❏ 1 bunch hornwort
- ❏ 3 Amazon swordplants
- ❏ 6 aponogeton instant bulbs

Index

G